California Seashore & Wildlife

Written and Illustrated
by Todd Telander

FALCONGUIDES®

GUILFORD, CONNECTICUT
HELENA, MONTANA

AN IMPRINT OF GLOBE PEQUOT PRESS

To my wife, Kirsten, my children, Miles and Oliver, and my parents, all of whom have supported and encouraged me through the years.

To buy books in quantity for corporate use
or incentives, call **(800) 962-0973**
or e-mail **premiums@GlobePequot.com**.

MIX
Paper from
responsible sources
FSC® C005010
www.fsc.org

FALCONGUIDES®

Copyright © 2014 Morris Book Publishing, LLC
Illustrations copyright © 2014 Todd Telander

FalconGuides is an imprint of Globe Pequot Press.
Falcon, FalconGuides, and Outfit Your Mind are registered trademarks of Morris Book Publishing, LLC.

Illustrations: Todd Telander
Project Editor: Staci Zacharski
Text Design: Sheryl P. Kober
Layout Artist: Sue Murray

Library of Congress Cataloging-in-Publication Data is available on file.

ISBN 978-0-7627-8183-6

Printed in the United States of America

10 9 8 7 6 5 4 3 2 1

Contents

Introduction. vii

Notes about the Species Accounts viii

Useful Scientific Terms x

Mammals 1

    Opossums 2

    Bats 3

    Rabbits, Hares, and Pika. 5

    Squirrels, Marmots, and Chipmunks 9

    Beavers 14

    Mice and Rats 15

    Large Rodents. 17

    Coyotes and Foxes 18

    Bears. 22

    Raccoon and Ringtail 23

    Skunks, Weasels, and Otters 25

    Cats 33

    Hoofed Mammals. 35

    Whales and Dolphins 41

    Sea Lions and Seals. 43

Birds 45

Nonpasserines 45

    Ducks and Geese 46

    Quails 51

    Grebes. 52

    Cormorants 54

    Pelicans 55

Herons and Egrets 56

Vultures 59

Hawks and Eagles 60

Falcons 63

Cranes 64

Plovers 65

Oystercatchers 66

Avocets 67

Sandpipers and Phalaropes 68

Gulls and Terns 72

Murres 75

Pigeons and Doves 76

Cuckoos 78

Owls 79

Hummingbirds 82

Kingfishers 83

Woodpeckers 84

Passerines 87

Flycatchers 88

Jays and Crows 90

Swallows 95

Chickadees and Titmice 96

Nuthatches 98

Creepers 99

Wrens 100

Kinglets 102

Thrushes 103

Mockingbirds, Catbirds, and Thrashers 106

Waxwings 107

Wood Warblers 108

Sparrows, Buntings. 111
Tanagers, Grosbeaks 115
Blackbirds, Orioles, and Grackles 116
Finches 118

Reptiles 119
Lizards. 120
Snakes. 127
Turtles 134

Amphibians. 135
Frogs. 136
Toads 138
Salamanders and Newts 140

Fish 145
Freshwater Fish 146
Sharks and Rays. 150
Saltwater Fish 151

Butterflies 163
Swallowtails and Parnassians 164
Sulfurs and Whites 166
Gossamer-Wings 169
Brushfoot Butterflies. 170

Moths. 175
Giant Silk Moths. 176
Sphinx Moths and Hawk Moths. 178
Tiger Moths 179

Seashore Invertebrates. 180
   Crabs, Lobsters, and Shrimp 181
   Octopus, Squid, and Anemone 187
   Sea Star 190
   Sea Urchins. 191
   Mussels 192

   Index. 193
   About the Author/Illustrator. 196

Introduction

Welcome to the Golden State! Home to an abundance of fascinating wildlife, California is the third largest state in the Union and stretches more than 800 miles from Mexico to Oregon, crossing 10 degrees of latitude. Between its extensive coastline and the high peaks of the Sierra Nevada, nearly every habitat type is accounted for. There is the barren desert of the southeast, the alpine lakes and meadows surrounding to Mount Whitney (the tallest peak in the contiguous United States), the lush redwood forests of the northwest, and the fertile Central Valley, with its Mediterranean-style climate. Living in this varied region are multitudes of mammals, birds, reptiles, amphibians, fish, butterflies, and seashore invertebrates, including some species found nowhere else in the continental United States, such as the Yellow-billed Magpie and the Arboreal Salamander. This guide is meant to be an overview of the vast diversity of wildlife in California, an introduction to some of the most common and distinct species that call this land home, and a starting point for your exploration of this unique state.

Notes about the Species Accounts

Names

Both the common name and the scientific name are included for each entry. Since common names tend to vary regionally, and there may be more than one common name for each species, the universally accepted scientific name of genus and species (such as *Nucifraga columbiana* for the Clark's Nutcracker) is more reliable to be certain of identification. Also, you can often learn interesting facts about an animal by understanding the English translation of its Latin name. For instance, the genus name, *Nucifraga,* derives from the Latin *nucis,* meaning "nut," and *fraga,* meaning "to break."

Size

Most measurements of size refer to overall length: nose to tail tip. For animals with very long tails, antennae, or other appendages, those measurements may be given separately from those of the body. Butterfly and moth measurements refer to wingspan. Size may vary considerably within a species (due to age, sex, or environmental conditions), so use a measurement as a general guide, not a rule.

Range

Range refers to the geographical area where a species is likely to be found, such as northern California, southern California, Sierra Nevada, Central Valley, etc. Some species may be found throughout their range, whereas others prefer very specific habitats within that range. Also mentioned under this heading is the season during which the species is present in California. For migratory birds, and for some butterflies, the season is the time when the greatest number of individuals is found. Some species are year-round residents, some may spend only summers or winters, and some may be transient, only stopping during the spring or fall migrations. Even if only part of the year is indicated for a species, be aware that there may be individuals that arrive earlier or remain longer than the given timeframe. Most land-dwelling animals are year-round residents. Some fish may arrive in seasonal migrations.

Habitat

An animal's habitat is one of the first clues to its identification. Note the environment (including vegetation, climate, elevation, substrate, presence or absence of water) where you see an animal and compare it with the description listed. Some common habitats in California include deserts, coastal dunes, shorelines, open ocean, redwoods, foothills, alpine areas, chaparral, rivers and streams, urban areas, and grasslands.

Illustrations

The illustrations show adult animals in the coloration they most likely have in California. Many species show variation in different geographical areas, different seasons, or between the sexes. Birds show this variety most often, so I have illustrated males and females when they look different. Other variations, such as seasonal color changes in some mammals and variable patterns in fish, are described in the text.

Useful Scientific Terms

I have, for the most part, used familiar language to describe the animals in this book, but there are occasions when it made more sense to use terms developed by the scientific community, especially when referring to body parts. In particular, terms and characteristics associated with birds, reptiles, amphibians, fish, and butterflies are described below.

Birds

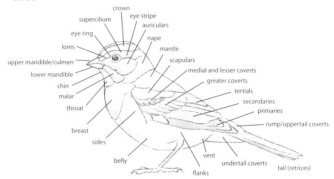

LIzards

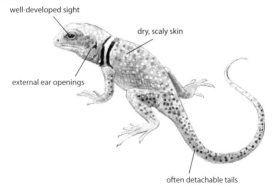

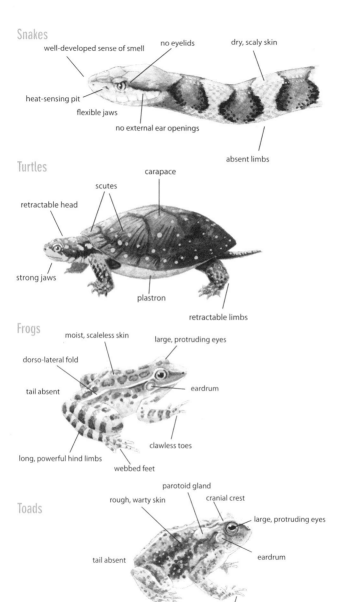

Snakes

well-developed sense of smell

no eyelids

dry, scaly skin

heat-sensing pit

flexible jaws

no external ear openings

absent limbs

Turtles

scutes

carapace

retractable head

strong jaws

plastron

retractable limbs

Frogs

moist, scaleless skin

large, protruding eyes

dorso-lateral fold

tail absent

eardrum

clawless toes

long, powerful hind limbs

webbed feet

Toads

parotoid gland

rough, warty skin

cranial crest

large, protruding eyes

tail absent

eardrum

weak hind legs

clawless toes

Salamanders

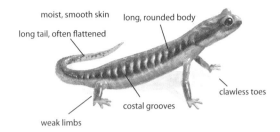

moist, smooth skin

long, rounded body

long tail, often flattened

clawless toes

costal grooves

weak limbs

Fish

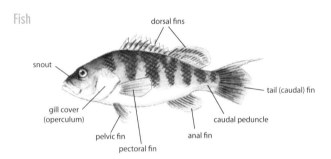

dorsal fins

snout

tail (caudal) fin

gill cover (operculum)

caudal peduncle

pelvic fin

anal fin

pectoral fin

Butterflies

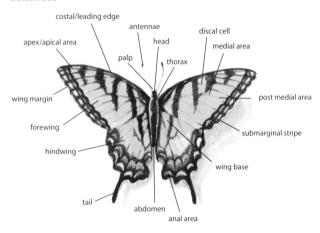

costal/leading edge

antennae

discal cell

apex/apical area

head

medial area

palp

thorax

wing margin

post medial area

forewing

submarginal stripe

hindwing

wing base

tail

abdomen

anal area

MAMMALS

Virginia Opossum, *Didelphis virginiana*
Family Didelphidae (Opossums)
Size: 30" with tail
Range: Lower elevations throughout California
Habitat: Woodlands, riparian zones, urban areas with trees, farms

The Virginia opossum is a marsupial, meaning it bears premature young that develop in an external pouch, and is the only member of this group in North America. It is stocky, with relatively small limbs, a pointed snout, and a long, round, hairless tail. Its color is mottled grayish with a white face and dark ears. It is nocturnal, mostly solitary, and reasonably adept at swimming and climbing. It has a highly varied diet that includes nuts, fruit, insects, small animals, and carrion. Opossums have a curious habit of feigning death when under attack, then carrying on as normal once safe.

Big Brown Bat, *Eptesicus fuscus*
Family Vespertilionidae (Vespertilionid Bats)
Size: 5" with tail
Range: Throughout California
Habitat: A wide variety, including woodlands, buildings, and caves

As a group, bats are the only mammals that truly fly, using wings composed of a thin membrane stretched across elongated forearms and fingers. The widely distributed big brown bat is fairly large, with fur that is brown above, lighter below, with blackish wing membranes. There is a fleshy projection at the base of the ear (the tragus), which is short and rounded. Big brown bats are nocturnal, roosting by day in dark, secluded areas such as caves or old buildings. They emerge at night to forage for beetles and other insects, locating them primarily by echolocation, emitting high-pitched chirps and receiving reflected sound with their complex, large ears.

Brazilian Free-tailed Bat, *Tadarida brasiliensis*
Family Molossidae (Free-tailed Bats)
Size: About 4" with tail
Range: Throughout California
Habitat: Caves, buildings, and surrounding environs

Also known as the Mexican free-tailed bat or guano bat, the Brazilian free-tailed bat is small, with narrow wings and a tail that projects freely about halfway past the interfemoral membrane, a patch of skin that stretches between the legs. The fur is rich brown, slightly darker above than below, and the wings are blackish. The ears are broad, reaching forward on the face, and the upper snout is wrinkled. Brazilian free-tailed bats emerge from roosting sites at night in large groups and forage for a variety of insects, using echolocation to zero in on prey. These bats are among the most numerous mammals in the United States, famous for gathering in enormous concentrations in caves in New Mexico and for the deep deposits of guano accumulated in those caves.

American Pika, *Ochotona princeps*
Family Ochotonidae (Pikas)
Size: About 8"
Range: Mountainous California
Habitat: Rocky slopes at high altitudes

The pika is a small, plump animal related to rabbits. It has a rela-tively large head, rounded ears, and a tiny tail that is usually not visible in the field. Its fur is thick and pale grayish brown. It is often detected by its high-pitched, squeaking call. Pikas make tunnels through the snow in winter that leave traces on the ground upon snowmelt. Active during the day, mostly solitary and moving about in slow bounds, pikas forage on grasses and herbs, which they store in large piles like hay for lean winter months.

Black-tailed Jackrabbit, *Lepus californicus*
Family Leporidae (Rabbits and Hares)
Size: About 23"
Range: Throughout California
Habitat: Prairies, open sageland, meadows

The black-tailed jackrabbit is a large, lanky hare with relatively long legs and huge, black-tipped ears. The color is gray brown, paler underneath, with a white tail that has a black stripe on top that extends onto the rump. The similar white-tailed jackrabbit has no dark color on the upper tail and inhabits mountains of eastern California. Jackrabbits are mostly nocturnal and solitary, highly alert, and able to elude predators with exceptionally fast runs and high jumps. They forage on grass and other vegetation, but may be limited to bark and buds in winter.

Desert Cottontail, *Sylvilagus audubonii*
Family Leporidae (Rabbits and Hares)
Size: 14"
Range: Central and southern California
Habitat: Drier areas; brush, thickets, upland fields

The desert cottontail is a relatively small rabbit, colored gray-brown with a reddish-brown patch on the back of the neck, a short, rounded, white tail (hence the common name), and long ears. The eyes are quite large, and the rear feet are long and powerful. The cottontails' high rate of reproduction and general abundance make them an important food source for carnivorous wildlife. Desert cottontails are mostly nocturnal, but can be seen feeding at almost any time for grasses, herbs, branches, and bark. The rabbits never stray too far from brushy cover or their burrows.

Brush Rabbit, *Sylvilagus bachmani*
Family Leporidae (Rabbits and Hares)
Size: 13"
Range: Western regions of California
Habitat: Dense, brushy areas

The brush rabbit is a smaller version of the desert cottontail, with a preference for thick brush in which to hide. Its fur is coarse; the color is brownish-gray overall. Its ears are relatively small and the tail is grayish brown and inconspicuous, unlike the white of the cottontail. Brush rabbits are secretive, foraging mostly during the night on all matter of vegetation, including twigs, grasses, bulbs, tubers, and leaves. As a defense they remain motionless, or run for the cover of brush, tunnels, or trees, and may be heard thumping their hind legs on the ground.

Western Gray Squirrel, *Sciurus griseus*
Family Sciuridae (Squirrels)
Size: 18" with tail
Range: Throughout most of California
Habitat: Mixed hardwood forests, parks, suburbs

The widespread and common western gray squirrel, also known as the California gray squirrel, is social, arboreal, and relatively large. It has a long, very bushy tail and large eyes. Its color is gray, sometimes with a brownish cast, and whitish below, with pale eye rings. Its tail is edged with white-tipped hairs. Active most times of the day, these squirrels forage for nuts, fruits, seeds, insects, eggs, and fungi, and may store nuts in ground caches. Ubiquitous in rural yards and parks, they use tree cavities to nest in, or may build large nests of twigs and leaves high in a tree.

Northern Flying Squirrel, *Glaucomys sabrinus*
Family Sciuridae (Squirrels)
Size: 16" with tail
Range: Northern and eastern California
Habitat: Coniferous or deciduous woodlands, oak stands

The unusual northern flying squirrel is small, designed to glide (not fly) from tree to tree or from tree to ground. Flaps of skin connect the front and rear feet; when outstretched, these flaps allow the squirrel to glide more than 100 feet and make a delicate landing. The color is grayish brown, darker along the flanks, and whitish below. Northern flying squirrels are active at night and are highly social, with several individuals sometimes sharing a nest site in a tree cavity or external structure. They forage for nuts, fruit, insects, fungus, and eggs, and store food in tree cavities for winter use.

Yellow-bellied Marmot, *Marmota flaviventris*
Family Sciuridae (Squirrels)
Size: About 24" with tail (males larger than females)
Range: Mountainous eastern California
Habitat: Rocky slopes and boulders at high elevation

The yellow-bellied marmot is a heavy, roundish ground squirrel with a medium-length, somewhat bushy tail and small ears. Its thick fur is pale tan-brown overall, with a yellowish belly and pale patches on the front of the face. Found alone or in groups, marmots are active during the day, perching atop boulders or foraging for herbs, grasses, and seeds. They are often seen at the highest mountain summits, and undergo long winter hibernations in underground burrows.

California Ground Squirrel, *Otospermophilus beecheyi*
Family Sciuridae (Squirrels)
Size: About 18" with tail
Range: Throughout most of California except for the southeastern desert area
Habitat: Fields, open woodlands, rocky area

The California ground squirrel is fairly common in open spaces throughout California. These squirrels are of medium length with bushy tails. The fur is speckled in shades of brown, gray, and white, with a darker, forward-pointing V-shaped patch along the back, and whitish patches along the sides to the base of the neck. The underside is paler, there are prominent white eye rings, and the tail is mottled or striped in the body colors. These squirrels are active during the day, sunning themselves or foraging for a wide variety of food including nuts, seeds, berries, roots, and insects. They form loose colonies with extensive burrow systems, which they excavate, and each individual has its own entrance, to which it will retreat to when in danger.

Least Chipmunk, *Tamias minimus*
Family Sciuridae (Squirrels)
Size: About 8"
Range: Northeastern and east-central California
Habitat: Arid, high-elevation open forests to lowland sagebrush and rocky areas

The smallest chipmunk in North America, but similar in body shape to other chipmunks, the least chipmunk has a small body, large head and eyes, and a long, bushy tail. The most obvious field mark are the white and dark brown stripes across the head and along the back. Much geographical variation exists, but typically its sides are orange-brown, the underparts are pale gray, and its tail is mottled with body colors, often striped with black near the base. The chipmunk usually holds its tail in a vertical position when running. Least chipmunks are active during the day from spring to fall, busily collecting nuts, berries, grasses, and insects, using an extendable cheek pouch to carry extra food for storage. They nest in burrows, under logs, or in trees, and spend the winter in a partial hibernation underground, where they periodically awaken to nibble on bits of cached food. They often visit campsites for food and can be quite vocal, emitting a high-pitched *chip*.

American Beaver, *Castor canadensis*
Family Castoridae (Beavers)
Size: 28" body; 10" tail
Range: Northern and extreme southeastern California
Habitat: Ponds, lakes, streams with adjacent woodlands

Once nearly extirpated due to hunting and trapping for pelts, this largest of North American rodents now covers most of its original range. The beaver is heavy and compact, with webbed rear feet, large front incisors, and a long, dexterous, scaled, flattened tail. Its color is dark brown. Beavers are known for cooperative construction of impressive dams and lodges made from trees they have felled. Their presence is often announced by a loud tail slap on the water. Mostly nocturnal, they eat the tender, inner bark of trees, as well as small branches and buds.

Ord's Kangaroo Rat, *Dipodomys ordii*
Family Heteromyidae (Pocket Mice and Kangaroo Rats)
Size: Body about 4"; tail 5.5"
Range: Far northeastern and east-central California
Habitat: Lowland prairies and scrublands with sandy soils

One of several species of kangaroo rat found across the arid West, the Ord's kangaroo rat occupies the largest range and is one of the smaller varieties. It is a compact rodent with a relatively large head, a long tail with a bushy distal portion, and oversize rear feet, akin to a kangaroo. Its color is buff to rusty brown, with white lateral stripes across the lower body and the middle of the tail. Mostly nocturnal and somewhat solitary, kangaroo rats spend the day in their burrows. They hop about, kangaroo-style, foraging for plants, seeds, and insects. They are well adapted to dry conditions, and receive most of the water they need through their food.

Deer Mouse, *Peromyscus maniculatus*
Family Cricetidae (New World Rats and Mice)
Size: Body 4"; tail 3"
Range: Throughout California
Habitat: Highly variable: grasslands, woodland, mountains, brushlands

The deer mouse is common and widespread, occurring in a wide range of habitats, and can vary in size and color depending on region. Its body shape is typical of mice, with a small body, pointed snout, large, black eyes, and large ears. Its tail is thin and varies in length, but is typically slightly shorter than the body. Color ranges from grayish to brown or orange-brown above, with white undersides and on the lower part of the face. The tail is dark above, sharply contrasting with white below. Deer mice are most commonly active during the night, emerging from daytime refuges of burrows or under rocks and stumps, scampering along the ground, in brush, or in trees gathering nuts, fruits, grasses, or insects. These mice will store extra food in a hidden cache to eat during lean winter months, since they do not hibernate.

Porcupine, *Erethizon dorsatum*
Family Erethizontidae (Porcupine)
Size: About 28" with tail
Range: Central and eastern California
Habitat: Forests, thickets

The porcupine is a primarily arboreal, chunky, lackadaisical rodent with small limbs, a bushy tail, and thousands of pointed barbed quills, which serve as its only defense. Its color is dark brown to blackish. Found alone or in groups, it is mostly nocturnal but can be seen at all times of the day, especially perched in trees. They feed on all types of plant matter, including buds, branches, bark, roots, and leaves.

Coyote, *Canis latrans*
Family Canidae (Coyotes and Foxes)
Size: 4' with tail
Range: Throughout California
Habitat: Open country, scrub, grassland

The coyote is an intelligent and adaptable canid that has been able to survive in a wide variety of habitats and in spite of persecution by humans. It looks like an average-size dog, with a long, thin muzzle and pointed ears. The color can range from gray to light brown or reddish. It has a bushy tail that is held low or between the legs. Coyotes hunt alone or in small packs, primarily during the night. Their diet is varied, and they scavenge for anything edible, including rodents, rabbits, snakes, berries, insects, and carrion.

Gray Fox, *Urocyon cinereoargenteus*
Family Canidae (Coyotes and Foxes)
Size: 3' with tail
Range: Throughout California
Habitat: Open woodlands, brush, suburban areas

The gray fox is a small, stealthy, nimble canid with a bushy tail and the ability to climb trees using its short, curved, retractable claws. Its fur is gray and occasionally speckled with white above, reddish along the sides and legs, with a black streak down the back and tail ending in a black tail tip. The muzzle is thin and small, while the ears are comparatively large. They are mostly solitary and nocturnal, and have a varied diet that includes rabbits, rodents, insects, nuts, and fruit.

Red Fox, *Vulpes vulpes*
Family Canidae (Coyotes and Foxes)
Size: 38" with tail
Range: Central and eastern California
Habitat: Open woodlands, fields, brushy areas; may approach urban centers

Like other foxes, the red fox is wily, secretive, adaptable, and dog-like, with a small muzzle, large ears, and a bushy tail. It is rusty red above, white or gray below, with black "stockings" on the legs and a white-tipped tail. Color variations may include black or slate gray fur, or a dark cross may be visible along the shoulders. Red foxes are solitary hunters and are most active at night or in the twilight hours, seeking the shelter of a den during the day. They feed on small mammals, insects, carrion, plants, and berries; sometimes performing a dramatic leaping pounce to catch rodents.

Kit Fox, *Vulpes macrotis*
Family Canidae (Coyotes and Foxes)
Size: 28" with tail
Range: Most of California except northwestern and central coastal regions
Habitat: Sandy arid areas, prairies, sagebrush

California's smallest canid, and the only one found in desert regions, the kit fox is a diminutive, house cat-size fox with comparatively large ears and a delicate face. Its color is pale reddish brown, mottled with gray above and lighter below. The tail has a black tip. It is primarily nocturnal, hunting for small mammals, insects, and reptiles, but the kit fox will also take carrion if available. It retreats to a den or burrow during the day. Some consider the kit fox to be the same species as the slightly larger swift fox of the Great Plains.

American Black Bear, *Ursus americanus*
Family Ursidae (Bears)
Size: 3' tall at the shoulder; 6' tall standing (males larger than females)
Range: Sierra Nevada and northern coastal ranges of California
Habitat: Forests, mountain valleys, open range

Although the smallest bear in North America, the American black bear is still heavy (up to 600 pounds) and lumbering, with thick (but not humped) shoulders, short legs, and small ears and tail. There is variation across its range, but in California its color is black or cinnamon brown, with a light brown muzzle and sometimes a white patch on its chest. Black bears feed mostly at night, covering large areas of land while foraging for plants, roots, berries, grubs, and occasionally small animals, fish, and carrion. The black bear is usually solitary, except in mating season or in family units composed of cubs and a mother. The bear spends most of the winter hibernating in a den, but can be aroused quickly.

Ringtail, *Bassariscus astutus*
Family Procyonidae (Ringtail, Raccoon)
Size: About 30" with tail
Range: Most of California except the Central Valley region
Habitat: Rocky deserts, forests

The ringtail is small and secretive, with delicate features, big, dark eyes, and a long, bushy tail. Although sometime referred to as the ringtail cat, it is not related to cats but allied more closely with raccoons. Its color is light brown above, paler below, with a striped black-and-white tail. Mostly nocturnal, it is usually found alone or in pairs. Ringtails are very agile climbers, using their long tails and flexible ankles to navigate through trees and rocks. They forage for both plants and animals, with a diet that includes berries, insects, birds, and small mammals.

Raccoon, *Procyon lotor*
Family Procyonidae (Ringtails and Raccoons)
Size: 34" with tail
Range: Throughout California
Habitat: Woodlands, streams or lakesides, urban areas

The raccoon is highly adaptable, equally at home in remote forests or urban centers. It is stocky and heavy, with a short, masked face and a bushy coat. Its color is pale gray mixed with black, with a tail ringed in black and gray. Incredibly dexterous fingers allow it to undo knots and even work doorknobs. Raccoons are primarily nocturnal and may be seen alone or in small groups. They prefer to feed near a water source, often dipping their food in water first, and will eat just about anything, including fruits, nuts, insects, fish, crayfish, and worms.

Sea Otter, *Enhydra lutris*
Family Mustelidae (Weasels and Otters)
Size: Up to 5'8" with tail
Range: Along the California coastline
Habitat: Near-shore marine waters, kelp beds, beaches

The gregarious, playful sea otter is the smallest marine mammal. Once nearly extinct due to exploitation by the fur trade, stable populations are now found along the California coast, but the species is still threatened. Almost entirely aquatic, it has a sinuous body with a rudderlike tail, and rear legs used as flippers. Its thick, dark brown fur, which it grooms scrupulously, provides insulation against the cool Pacific waters, since the sea otter lacks the layer of blubber found in other marine mammals. Sea otters dive for shellfish, sea urchins and fish, then float on their backs to feed, often using a stone to crack apart the shell surrounding prey such as abalone. They use the shelter of kelp beds to hide from predators, and as support while resting or sleeping.

Northern River Otter, *Lontra canadensis*
Family Mustelidae (Weasels and Otters)
Size: 4' with tail
Range: Northern and central California
Habitat: Areas near streams, lakes, or estuaries

The river otter is large, curious, and playful, with a mostly aquatic lifestyle. It is elongate and sinuous, with small ears, webbed feet, and a long, somewhat thickened tail to aid in swimming. Its fur is thick, dark brown above and pale gray below and across the lower face. River otters are social and often travel in small family groups. They hunt primarily in the water for fish, amphibians, or aquatic invertebrates. They live in burrows near water and form well-used trails along the shore or between water sources.

Marten, *Martes americana*
Family Mustelidae (Weasels and Otters)
Size: About 25" with tail
Range: Sierra Nevada and mountainous northern California
Habitat: Forested areas

The marten is elongate and slender, with a long tail, short legs, and a pointed snout. It is stockier than a weasel, with larger, rounded ears, but is much smaller than a fisher, with whom it shares a similar range. Its color is golden brown, with a buff or orange patch on its throat and chest. Numbers in this species have been severely reduced by trappers seeking the luxurious pelts. Martens are nocturnal and solitary. Adept climbers, they hunt small mammals in trees or on the ground, and may feed on nuts and berries when available.

Fisher, *Martes pennanti*
Family Mustelidae (Weasels and Otters)
Size: About 34" with tail
Range: Sierra Nevada and mountainous northern California
Habitat: Forested areas

The fisher is basically weasel-shaped, with an elongate body, short legs, and a long, bushy tail, but is heavier and thicker. Its fur is dense and colored a rich, dark brown tipped with white, giving the fisher a grizzled or frosted, glistening appearance. Its numbers have been severely reduced due to hunting for pelts. Fishers are solitary animals, active day or night. They are excellent climbers and agile predators, preferring thick forests and fallen timber. They hunt a wide variety of mammals and birds, even preying upon porcupines. They will also eat plants, berries, and carrion. Contrary to the common name, fishers rarely feed on fish.

Long-tailed Weasel, *Mustela frenata*
Family Mustelidae (Weasels and Otters)
Size: 14" with tail
Range: Most of California except the far southeastern region
Habitat: Woodlands; fields with brushy cover, often near water

The long-tailed weasel is a small, wily, elongate, long-necked predator, and one of California's smallest meat eaters. It is reddish brown, with buff-colored underparts and throat, and a black tip on its long tail. It is nocturnal and solitary, an excellent climber, and, due to its thin, sinuous shape and short legs, the long-tailed weasel can slip into burrows to attack rodents living within. Long-tailed weasels also eat rabbits, birds, eggs, and fish. To den, they use the existing burrows of other, similar-size rodents.

American Mink, *Neovison vison*
Family Mustelidae (Weasels and Otters)
Size: 20" with tail
Range: Northern and central California
Habitat: Coastal areas, streams, marshes

The American mink is elongate and short-legged, with a long tail, webbed feet, and a semiaquatic lifestyle. Its luxurious pelt is dark blackish brown; mink sometimes have a whitish area around the mouth and may have pale spotting on the underside. Mink are mostly nocturnal and solitary, are excellent swimmers, and never stray too far from a water source. They are carnivores, eating aquatic animals and invertebrates, but will also take birds, eggs, and rabbits.

Striped Skunk, *Mephitis mephitis*
Family Mephitidae (Skunks)
Size: 22" with tail
Range: Throughout California
Habitat: Woodlands, brush, suburban parks; usually near a water source

The striped skunk is known primarily for its ability to elude danger by spraying a noxious fluid from an anal duct. It is a stocky, weasel-like mammal with a long, bushy tail, and long front claws for digging. Its color is black, with broad white stripes running down its sides that merge into a white stripe on the upper part of the tail. Usually solitary, striped skunks stay in their dens during the day and forage at night. Being omnivorous, they eat a wide variety of foods including fruit, nuts, insects, small mammals, and eggs.

Western Spotted Skunk, *Spilogale gracilis*
Family Mephitidae (Skunks)
Size: 18" with tail
Range: Throughout California
Habitat: Brushy open woodlands, coastal scrub, grasslands; usually near a water source

The western spotted skunk is smaller than the striped skunk, but shares its defensive ability to spray a noxious liquid from ducts near its anus. It is weasel-like, with fine, soft fur, a thick, bushy tail, and long claws. Its color is black, with variable and irregular white spotting and striping on the head and back, and a white-tipped tail. Solitary and nocturnal, these skunks stay in dens during the day. They can climb trees but mostly forage on the ground, eating a variety of foods including fruit, insects, small mammals, birds, and eggs.

Mountain Lion (Cougar), *Puma concolor*
Family Felidae (Cats)
Size: 7' body; 2.5' tail (males larger than females)
Range: Throughout California
Habitat: Woodlands (both open and dense), brush

The mountain lion (also known as the cougar or puma) is a huge (about 125 pounds), reclusive, powerful cat. It has a long tail, and its fur is a blend of tawny browns, tans, and grays, paler on the underside and white on the chest and throat. Its tail tip is dark brown, as are the backs of its ears and marks on its muzzle. Mountain lions are mostly solitary, except during breeding season or when with kittens. They hunt using stealth, waiting on rocky ledges or trees for prey to pass, or slinking through grass to ambush prey, which includes deer, elk, and smaller mammals.

Bobcat, *Lynx rufus*
Family Felidae (Cats)
Size: 28" body; 5" tail
Range: Most of California, except the Central Valley region
Habitat: A wide variety of habitats, including forests, riparian areas, and scrub

The bobcat is about double the size of a house cat, is well camouflaged, and has a very short, "bobbed" tail. Its face appears wide due to the long fur tufts below its ears, and the ears are tipped with short, black hairs. Its color is light brown to reddish above, pale or whitish below; its coat is spotted with dark brown or black that is sometimes streaked on the legs. Its tail is striped, and black along the top edge. Bobcats are typically active during early morning hours and after dusk, except in winter when they are active during the day. They hunt by stealth, ambushing their favored prey of rabbits, other small mammals, and birds.

Pronghorn, *Antilocapra americana*
Family Antilocapridae (Pronghorns)
Size: 4.5' (males larger than females)
Range: Eastern California
Habitat: Grassy plains, sagebrush

The pronghorn is the only member of its family, and bears a resemblance to the antelopes of the Old World. It is light brown with a white rump patch, belly and band about the neck. Its neck also has a darker brown band and dark facial patterning. Both sexes have rough, black, flattened horns, which curve at the tip and have a single, forward-projecting prong. The outer sheath of the horn is shed and regrown each year. Pronghorns are primarily active during the morning and afternoon, are found singly or in small groups, and forage on grasses, herbaceous plants, and sagebrush. When pursued, pronghorns can run up to 40 miles per hour, making them the fastest mammals in North America.

Bighorn Sheep, *Ovis canadensis*
Family Bovidae (Sheep, Goats)
Size: About 3' tall at the shoulder; body 6' long (males larger than females)
Range: Eastern California
Habitat: Rugged, mountainous areas

The bighorn sheep is the largest of the true sheep, and consists of subspecies found in the Rocky Mountains, the Sierra Nevada, and the desert Southwest. They are closely related to the dall sheep of Alaska and western Canada, but have larger horns. The bighorn is stocky, with a strong neck and shoulder, and is colored light brown to grayish with white rumps. The backs of the legs are also white. Both sexes have horns, but those of the male are much larger, curve in an arc to the back, and can weigh up to 25 pounds. The males use their horns in dramatic head-butting rituals during the mating season. Sure-footed and agile, bighorn sheep form groups and forage on all varieties of plants and tree branches; they are able to eat very dry and tough material.

Elk (Wapiti), *Cervus elaphus*
Family Cervidae (Deer, Elk, Moose)
Size: Body 8'; tail 5" (males larger than females)
Range: Northwestern California; isolated areas of south-central California
Habitat: Mountainous forests, high meadows, coastal woodlands

The elk is a large, gregarious member of the deer family with a pale, stubby tail. Its fur is short in the summer, longer in the winter, and colored pale rusty brown with a darker neck and face. The rump is buff-colored surrounded by dark brown fur. Males have a shaggy, dark mane about the neck, and large antlers with tines growing from a central beam. Usually active in the morning and evening, elk form large herds of up to hundreds of individuals. They browse for grasses, herbs, branches, and the tender inner bark of trees.

Mule Deer, *Odocoileus hemionus*
Family Cervidae (Deer, Elk, Moose)
Size: 6' (males larger than females)
Range: Throughout California
Habitat: Variable, including forests, chaparral, bushy grasslands

The mule deer is quite common throughout its range, and derives its common name from its very large, mulelike ears. Its color is gray-brown in winter and rusty brown in summer, with a white throat, muzzle, and belly. Depending on the region, its tail may have a black tip or have black on the top surface. Males have antlers that are evenly forked (no tines from a central beam, as is found on the white-tailed deer). In summer, the antlers are covered in velvet. Mule deer are active at twilight hours, moving in small groups or singly, browsing for tree branches, grasses, and herbs.

White-tailed Deer, *Odocoileus virginianus*
Family Cervidae (Deer)
Size: 6' body; 10" tail
Range: Northeastern California
Habitat: Dense forest, forest edges

North America's smallest deer, the white-tailed deer is a secretive resident of thick forests. It is very agile, fast, and able to outmaneuver most predators. The male has antlers with a main beam that supports smaller prongs. The color of its fur is reddish brown, with a white belly and throat. When alarmed, the white-tailed deer raises its tail, revealing the brilliant white underside, hence its colloquial name of "flagtail." White-tailed deer travel in small groups in summer, but in winter may congregate in larger herds. Being herbivores, they forage for grasses, herbs, and nuts.

Wild Boar (Feral Pig), *Sus scrofa*
Family Suidae (Hogs, Pigs)
Size: 4' body; 6" tail
Range: Scattered populations throughout California
Habitat: Forests, open woodlands, swamps

Wild boars are either feral populations of domesticated pigs, wild
boars introduced from Europe, or hybrids of the two. They have
stocky bodies with short, thin legs, and large heads with protruding snouts. They can achieve weights of up to 200 pounds,
and the male wild boar has canines enlarged into tusks. The hair
is bristly and thick, and varies in color from black to brownish to
white. Quick and quite aggressive, wild boars are active mostly
during the morning and evening, and can be found alone or in
groups. They forage on the move, digging up roots and tubers,
grazing on plants, and hunting insects.

Gray Whale, *Eschrichtius robustus*
Family Eschrichtiidae (Gray Whale)
Size: Up to 45'
Range: Coastal California
Habitat: Offshore marine waters

The gray whale, once severely threatened due to the whaling industry, is now relatively common off the California coast, and is a favorite of whale watchers as it often approaches close to boats and headlands. This huge marine mammal has a fairly narrow head (triangular from above), wide flippers, and a short hump on its back, followed by several smaller bumps along the back to the tail. The whale's wide flukes (tail flippers) are often raised out of the water when it dives. Its body is mottled deep to pale gray, and variously coated with barnacles and lice, especially on the upper head region. A member of the group known as baleen whales, gray whales don't have teeth, but rather a network of pleated tissue in their mouths that works as a filter to extract massive amounts of tiny marine organisms from the open ocean or the muddy bottom. They are most commonly seen singly or in small groups, methodically migrating to and from breeding areas in Mexico and summer feeding grounds in the Arctic.

Bottlenose Dolphin, *Tursiops truncatus*
Family Delphinidae (Ocean Dolphins)
Size: 8–12' (males larger than females)
Range: Coastal California
Habitat: Coastal waters, bays, estuaries, mouths of major rivers

The bottlenose dolphin is widespread in California's waters and across the globe in tropical oceans. Agile and playful, it travels in groups known as pods (sometimes containing more than one hundred individuals). The bottlenose is the dolphin most often seen at aquatic shows, or riding the wakes of ships. It is a sleek, flexible, marine mammal with a bottle-shaped snout, a triangular dorsal fin, and a blowhole for breathing at the top of its head. The skin is smooth, dark gray above, medium gray along the sides, whitish on the belly and throat, with some darker streaking forward and behind the eyes. Bottlenose dolphins prey mostly on fish and squid, which they hunt with the help of echolocation, chasing them down by swimming quickly.

California Sea Lion, *Zalophus californianus*
Family Otariidae (Sea Lions)
Size: Up to 7' (males larger than females)
Range: Coastal California, the offshore islands of southern California
Habitat: Rocky coastlines, marinas, dams, beaches

Perhaps the most recognizable pinniped, the California sea lion is often seen in busy harbors and can be trained to do tricks for shows. Sea lions differ from seals in that they have external ear flaps, long whiskers, swim by paddling their large front flippers, and can walk on land on their hind legs. California sea lions have short, dense fur that ranges from light brown to blackish. Females are slender in build, while males are larger, with robust necks and chests, and tall foreheads. When feeding, sea lions dive for minutes at a time in open water or along the bottom, hunting for a variety of fish and squid. They may also harass fishing vessels or gather at river mouths to hunt migrating fish. When onshore or hauled out onto a dock, sea lions form large, noisy groups. The female is illustrated.

Harbor Seal, *Phoca vitulina*
Family Phocidae (True Seals)
Size: Up to 6'
Range: Coastal California
Habitat: Offshore coastal waters, rocky or sandy beaches, lagoons, river mouths

Being members of the true seal family (as opposed to the sea lion family), harbor seals have earholes with no external flaps, relatively small front flippers with obvious claws, and move about on their bellies with their hind limbs lifted up. Although historically hunted extensively for their fur, harbor seals are quite common today, seen close to shore or hauled out on protected beaches and rocky outcrops. Sexes are similar in appearance, with plump, rounded bodies, large, black eyes, and a wide, short snouts. The color ranges geographically from silvery gray or light brown with dark spots to nearly black with whitish spots that may form rings. Equally comfortable on land or in water, harbor seals forage alone or in small groups by diving for fish and squid, propelled by their hind flippers and undulating bodies. When molting, they often form large aggregations at haul-out sites.

BIRDS:
NONPASSERINES

Canada Goose, *Branta canadensis*
Family Anatidae (Ducks, Geese)
Size: 27–35", depending on subspecies
Season: Winter
Habitat: Marshes, grasslands, public parks, golf courses

The Canada goose is California's most common goose, and is often found in suburban settings. It is vegetarian, foraging on land for grasses, seeds, and grain. In water, the goose forages by upending like the dabbling ducks. It has a heavy body with short, thick legs, and a long neck. Overall it is barred gray-brown with a white rear, with a short black tail, a black neck, and a white patch running under the neck to behind the eye. During flight, in which groups assume the classic V formation, the white across the rump makes a semicircular patch between the tail and back. Flight is powerful; the voice is a loud *honk*. The adult is illustrated.

Snow Goose, *Chen caerulescens*
Family Anatidae (Ducks, Geese)
Size: 28"
Season: Winter in the Sacramento Valley; a transient migrant elsewhere
Habitat: Grasslands, marshes

The snow goose forms huge, impressive flocks when visiting California during spring and fall migrations, during which the geese travel between the Arctic and southern North America and Mexico. It has two color forms: the "blue" and the more common "white." The white form is predominantly white, with black outer wing feathers and a pale yellowish wash to the face during summer. The blue form retains the white head and lower belly, but is otherwise dark slate gray or brownish gray. In both morphs, its bill is pink, thick at the base, and has a black patch where the mandibles meet. The legs of both morphs are pink. Snow geese feed mostly on the ground, eating shoots, roots, grains, and insects. The similar Ross's Goose is smaller, and has a shorter bill. The white morph adult is illustrated.

Mallard, *Anas platyrhynchos*
Family Anatidae (Ducks, Geese)
Size: 23"
Season: Year-round
Habitat: Virtually any water environment, parks, urban areas

The ubiquitous mallard is the most abundant duck in the Northern Hemisphere. It is a classic dabbling duck, plunging its head into the water with its tail up, searching for aquatic plants, animals, and snails, although it will also eat worms, seeds, insects, and even mice. Noisy and quacking, it is heavy but is a strong flier. The male has a dark head with green or blue iridescence, a white neck ring, and a large yellow bill. The underparts are pale, with a chestnut-brown breast. The female is plain brownish, with buff scalloped markings, and has a dark eye line and an orangey bill with a dark center. The speculum is blue on both sexes, and the tail coverts often curl upward. Mallards form huge floating flocks called "rafts." To achieve flight, the mallard lifts straight into the air without running. The breeding female (top) and breeding male (bottom) are illustrated.

Northern Pintail, *Anas acuta*
Family Anatidae (Ducks, Geese)
Size: 21"
Season: Winter
Habitat: Marshes, shallow lakes, coastal bays

Among the most abundant ducks in North America, the northern pintail is an elegant, slender dabbling duck with a long neck, small head, and narrow wings. In breeding plumage, the male has long, pointed central tail feathers. It is gray along the back and sides, with a brown head and a white breast. A white stripe extends from the breast along the back of the neck. The female is mottled brown-and-tan overall, with a light brown head. To feed, the northern pintail bobs its head into the water to capture aquatic invertebrates and plants from the muddy bottom. It rises directly out of the water to take flight. The breeding female (top) and breeding male (bottom) are illustrated.

Surf Scoter, *Melanitta perspicillata*
Family Anatidae (Ducks, Geese)
Size: 20"
Season: Winter along the Pacific Coast
Habitat: Coastal waters

The surf scoter is a stocky, large-headed, coastal diving duck with short, pointed wings and a thick-based, colorful bill. The male is black overall, with white patches at the back of the neck and on the forehead. Its eyes are light, and its bill is orange with white on the sides and round black spots in the white portions. The female is brownish overall, with a black cap, grayish bill, and faint white patches along the base of the bill and cheeks, and sometimes on the nape. Surf scoters dive for shellfish and crustaceans, propelled by their short wings. Because of their markings, they are sometimes called "skunk-headed ducks." The breeding female (top) and breeding male (bottom) are illustrated.

California Quail, *Callipepla californica*
Family Odontophoridae (New World Quails)
Size: 10"
Season: Year-round
Habitat: Open woodlands, shrubby areas, rural gardens

The California state bird, this elegant, gentle little ground bird has a curious, forward-projecting head plume and a short, curved bill. The male is grayish overall, with pale barring and scaling on the sides, flanks, and belly. His head is boldly marked with a rusty crown, black face, and white stripes above the eyes and around the chin. The female lacks the bold head pattern, and her plume is much smaller. California quail travel in groups, picking the ground for seeds, insects, and berries. The voice is a squawking, throaty, usually three-noted *caw-CAW-caw*, sometimes dubbed "chi-CA-go." They roost low in trees or brush. The adult male is illustrated.

51

Western Grebe, *Aechmophorus occidentalis*
Family Podicipedidae (Grebes)
Size: 25"
Season: Year-round
Habitat: Shallow lakes, marshes, coastal waters

The western grebe is elegant and large, with an extremely long, thin neck and a long, pointed, greenish-yellow bill with an upturned lower mandible. It is slate gray above and crisp white below. The head and neck are cleanly divided black and white, with black encompassing the red eyes (unlike the similar Clark's grebe). Western grebes dive for fish and aquatic invertebrates, and voice a high-pitched, rattling *kreek-kreek*. They rarely take flight, but when they do, takeoff is preceded by a long, labored run across the water surface. The Western grebe was once considered the same species as the Clark's grebe. The breeding adult is illustrated.

Pied-billed Grebe, *Podilymbus podiceps*
Family Podicipedidae (Grebes)
Size: 13"
Season: Year-round
Habitat: Freshwater ponds and lakes

The pied-billed grebe is small and secretive, lurking in sheltered waters and diving for small fish, leeches, snails, and crawfish. When alarmed, or to avoid predatory snakes and hawks, it has the habit of sinking until only its head is above water, remaining that way until danger has passed. It is brownish overall and slightly darker above, with a tiny tail and short wings. The breeding adult has a conspicuous dark ring around the middle of the bill, which is missing in winter plumage. Pied-billed grebes nest on floating mats of vegetation. The breeding adult is illustrated.

Double-crested Cormorant, *Phalacrocorax auritus*
Family Phalacrocoracidae (Cormorants)
Size: 32"
Season: Year-round
Habitat: Open waters

Named for the two long white plumes that emerge from behind
its eyes during breeding season, the double-crested cormorant
is an expert swimmer that dives underwater to chase down fish.
Because its plumage lacks oils to repel water, it will stand with
wings outstretched to dry after a dive. It is all black, with a pale
glossy cast on the back and wings. Its eyes are bright green, its bill
is thin and hooked, and its throat patch and lores are yellow. The
breeding adult is illustrated.

Brown Pelican, *Pelecanus occidentalis*
Family Pelecanidae (Pelicans)
Size: 50"
Season: Year-round
Habitat: Coastal waters

The majestic brown pelican enlivens the coastal waters with its spectacular feeding process of plunge-diving for fish, headfirst, from some height. Pelicans often fly in formation inches from incoming swells, gaining lift and rarely needing to flap their wings. It has a massive bill. Plumage is a bleached gray-brown overall with a white head and neck. In breeding plumage, the head is pale yellow with a brown-red nape patch and a black stripe down the back of the neck. The brown pelican is quite gregarious, and nests in trees or in slight depressions in the sand or rocks. The breeding adult is illustrated.

Great Blue Heron, *Ardea herodias*
Family Ardeidae (Herons, Egrets)
Size: 46"
Season: Year-round
Habitat: Most aquatic areas, including lakes, creeks, and marshes

The great blue heron is the largest heron in North America. Walking slowly through shallow water or fields, it stalks fish, crabs, and small vertebrates, catching them with its massive bill. With long legs and a long neck, it is blue-gray overall, with a white face and a heavy yellow-orange bill. The crown is black, with plumes of medium length. The front of the neck is white, with distinct black chevrons fading into breast plumes. In flight, the neck is tucked back and the wing beats are regular and labored. The adult is illustrated.

Snowy Egret, *Egretta thula*
Family Ardeidae (Herons, Egrets)
Size: 24"
Season: Year-round
Habitat: Open water, marshes, swamps

The snowy egret is all white, with lacy plumes across the back in breeding season. Its bill is slim and black, and its legs are black, with bright yellow feet. The juvenile has greenish legs with a yellow stripe along the front. The snowy egret forages for fish and frogs along the shore by moving quickly, shuffling to stir up prey that it then stabs with its bill. Sometimes it runs to pursue its prey. The bird's name can be remembered by keeping in mind that it wears yellow "boots" because it is "snowy." The breeding adult is illustrated.

Black-crowned Night Heron, *Nycticorax nycticorax*
Family Ardeidae (Herons, Egrets)
Size: 25"
Season: Year-round
Habitat: Marshes, swamps with wooded banks

The nocturnal black-crowned night heron is stocky and thick-necked, with a comparatively large head and a sharp, heavy, thick bill. It has pale gray wings, white underparts, and a black crown, back, and bill. Its eyes are piercing red, and its legs are yellow-orange. In breeding plumage it develops long white plumes on the rear of its head. During the day it roosts in groups, but at night it forages alone, waiting motionless for prey such as fish or crabs. It may even raid the nests of other birds. Its voice is composed of low-pitched barks and croaks. The adult is illustrated.

Turkey Vulture, *Cathartes aura*
Family Cathartidae (New World Vultures)
Size: 27"
Season: Year-round
Habitat: Open, dry country

The turkey vulture is known for its effortless, skilled soaring. It will often soar for hours, without flapping, rocking in the breeze on 6-foot wings that form an upright V shape, or dihedral angle. It has a black body and inner wing, with pale flight feathers and tail feathers that give it a noticeable two-toned appearance from below. Its tail is longish, and its feet extend no more than halfway past the base of the tail. Its head is naked, red, and small, so the bird appears almost headless in flight. The bill is strongly hooked to aid in tearing apart its favored prey, carrion. Juveniles have a dark gray head. Turkey vultures often roost in flocks and form groups around food or at a roadkill site. The adult is illustrated.

Sharp-shinned Hawk, *Accipiter striatus*
Family Accipitridae (Hawks, Eagles)
Size: 10–14" (females larger than males)
Season: Year-round
Habitat: Woodlands, bushy areas

The sharp-shinned hawk is North America's smallest accipiter, with a longish, squared tail and stubby, rounded wings. Its short wings allow for agile flight in tight, wooded quarters, where it quickly attacks small birds in flight. It is grayish above and light below, barred with pale rufous stripes. The eyes are set forward on the face to aid in the direct pursuit of prey. The juvenile is white below, streaked with brown. The sharp-shinned hawk may be confused with the larger Cooper's hawk. The adult is illustrated.

Red-tailed Hawk, *Buteo jamaicensis*
Family Accipitridae (Hawks, Eagles)
Size: 20"
Season: Year-round
Habitat: Open country, prairie

This widespread species is the most common buteo in the United States. It has broad, rounded wings and a stout, hooked bill. Its plumage is highly variable depending on geographic location. In general, its underparts are light, with darker streaking that forms a dark band across the belly. Its upperparts are dark brown, and the tail is rufous. Light spotting occurs along the scapulars. In flight, there are noticeable dark patches along the inner leading edges of the underwings. Red-tailed hawks glide down from perches, such as telephone poles and posts in open country, to catch rodents. They may also hover to spot prey. They are usually seen alone or in pairs. Voice is the familiar *keeer!* The western adult is illustrated.

Bald Eagle, *Haliaeetus leucocephalus*
Family Accipitridae (Hawks, Eagles)
Size: 30–40", female larger than male
Season: Year-round or winter
Habitat: Lakes, rivers with tall perches or cliffs

The bald eagle is a large raptor that is widespread but fairly uncommon. It eats fish or scavenges dead animals, and congregates in large numbers where food is abundant. Its plumage is dark brown, contrasting with its white head and tail. Juveniles show white splotching across the wings and breast. The yellow bill is large and powerful, and the talons are large and sharp. In flight, the eagle holds its wings fairly flat and straight, resembling a long plank. Bald eagles make huge nests of sticks high in trees. The adult is illustrated.

American Kestrel, *Falco sparverius*
Family Falconidae (Falcons)
Size: 10"
Season: Year-round
Habitat: Open country, urban areas

North America's most common falcon, the American kestrel is a robin-size falcon with long, pointed wings and tail. Fast in flight, it hovers above fields or dives from a perch on a branch or wire to capture small animals and insects. Its upperparts are rufous and barred with black, the wings are blue-gray, and the breast is buff or white and streaked with black spots. It has a gray crown and vertical patches of black down its face. The female has rufous wings and a barred tail. Also known as the sparrow hawk, the kestrel has a habit of flicking its tail up and down while perched. The adult male is illustrated.

63

Sandhill Crane, *Grus canadensis*
Family Gruidae (Cranes)
Size: 45"
Season: Winter
Habitat: Fields, shallow wetlands

The sandhill crane is tall, with long, strong legs, a long neck, and a long, straight bill. The long, thick tertial feathers create the distinctive bustles on the rears of all cranes. The top of the sandhill crane's head is covered by bare red skin. Plumage is gray overall, but may become spotted with rust-colored stains caused by preening with a bill stained by iron-rich mud. Traveling in flocks, the sandhill crane grazes in fields, gleaning grains, insects, and small animals, and returns to protected wetland areas in the evening to roost. The voice of the sandhill crane is a throaty, penetrating trumpeting sound. Unlike herons, it flies in groups with its neck extended. The adult is illustrated.

Killdeer, *Charadrius vociferus*
Family Charadriidae (Plovers)
Size: 10"
Season: Year-round
Habitat: Inland fields, farmlands, lakeshores, meadows

The killdeer gets its name from its piercing *kill-dee* call, which is often heard before the well-camouflaged plover is seen. Well adapted to human-altered environments, the killdeer is widespread and gregarious. It has long, pointed wings, a long tail, and a conspicuous double-banded breast. The upper parts are dark brown, the belly is white, and the head is patterned with a white supercilium and forehead. The tail is rusty orange with a black tip. In flight, there is a noticeable white stripe across the flight feathers. The killdeer is known for the classic "broken wing" display it uses to distract predators from its nest and young. The adult is illustrated.

Black Oystercatcher, *Haematopus bachmani*
Family Haematopodidae (Oystercatchers)
Size: 17.5"
Season: Year-round along Pacific Coast
Habitat: Rocky coastlines

The black oystercatcher is a large, strong shorebird with a thick neck, short tail, and long, laterally flattened, deep red-orange bill. The sexes are similar in appearance, with brownish-black plumage, thick legs, and yellow eyes with red orbital rings. They feed by picking and prying shellfish and marine invertebrates from rocky intertidal zones. Black oystercatchers are usually seen singly, climbing about on rocks or swimming offshore—they rarely visit sandy or muddy shores. The voice is a shrill, piercing *weep!* The adult is illustrated.

American Avocet, *Recurvirostra americana*
Family Recurvirostridae (Avocets)
Size: 18"
Season: Year-round
Habitat: Shallow wetlands, marshes

The elegant American avocet has a long, delicate, upturned black bill and long, thin, blue-gray legs. Its upperparts are patterned black and white, the belly is white, and the head and neck is light orange-brown punctuated by black eyes. The bill of the female is slightly shorter than that of the male, and has a greater bend. Nonbreeding adults have pale gray heads and necks. Avocets sweep their bills from side to side to stir up small crustaceans and insect larvae as they wade methodically through the shallows. They may even submerge their heads as the water deepens. They are adept swimmers and emit a *wheet!* call in alarm. The breeding female (top) and breeding male (bottom) are illustrated.

Willet, *Tringa semipalmatus*
Family Scolopacidae (Sandpipers, Phalaropes)
Size: 15"
Season: Winter
Habitat: Saltwater and freshwater wetlands, coastal beaches

The willet is a heavy shorebird with a stout bill and conspicuous black-and-white wing markings in flight. Plumage is overall mocha brown above and pale below, with extensive mottling in the breeding season. The willet has white lores and eye rings, and its plain gray legs are thick and sturdy. It is found singly or in scattered flocks, and picks or probes for crabs, crustaceans, and worms in the mud and sand. Its call is a loud *wil-let,* often uttered in flight. The winter adult is illustrated.

Marbled Godwit, *Limosa fedoa*
Family Scolopacidae (Sandpipers, Phalaropes)
Size: 18"
Season: Winter
Habitat: Coastal beaches, mudflats, marshes

As its name suggests, the marbled godwit is marbled, or barred, with dark across its buff body, although its underside lacks marbling when in winter plumage. Its long pinkish bill has a slight up-curved portion at the tip, where it becomes dark in color. Its legs are dark, and the underwing is a rich cinnamon color. It also has a light superciliary stripe above a dark eye line. Marbled godwits move about with slow, steady progress and probe in shallow water to find polychaete worms and crustaceans. Its call is a loud *god-WIT*. The nonbreeding adult is illustrated.

Ruddy Turnstone, *Arenaria interpres*
Family Scolopacidae (Sandpipers, Phalaropes)
Size: 9.5"
Season: Winter
Habitat: A wide variety of shoreline habitats, from rocky intertidal zones to beaches and mudflats

The gregarious, frenetic ruddy turnstone is a chunky, short-legged shorebird with a short, wedge-shaped bill. The breeding adult has ruddy and black upperparts, a white belly, and a complex pattern of black and white on the head. The nonbreeding bird is pale brown and black above, with drab head markings. Its stubby legs are orange. In flight, the bird is white below and strongly patterned light and dark above. Turnstones bustle about constantly to pick, pry, or probe for almost any food item. Indeed, the bird will "turn stones" to search for its prey. The nonbreeding adult (top) and breeding adult (bottom) are illustrated.

Sanderling, *Calidris alba*
Family Scolopacidae (Sandpipers, Phalaropes)
Size: 8"
Season: Winter
Habitat: Coastal beaches, mudflats

The sanderling is a common shorebird that runs back and forth following the incoming and outgoing surf, grabbing small invertebrates exposed by the waves. This small, active, squat sandpiper has a short bill and legs. In nonbreeding plumage, it is very pale above and white below, contrasting with its black legs and bill. The sanderling has a distinct black shoulder, and black on the leading edge of the wing. Females in breeding plumage are speckled brown above, while males develop rufous on the back, head, and neck. In flight, a white stripe on the upper wing is visible. Sanderlings may form large, foraging flocks, and even larger flocks while roosting. The nonbreeding adult is illustrated.

California Gull, *Larus californicus*
Family Laridae (Gulls, Terns)
Size: 21"
Season: Winter
Habitat: Coastal areas, lakes, rivers, prairie wetlands

The California gull is medium-size with a relatively thin, long bill. The breeding adult is medium blue gray above, with white edges to the tertial and secondary feathers, and is white below. Its primaries are black with white spotting, and the tail is white. Its head is rounded, the eyes are dark, and the bill is yellow orange with a black-and-red spot near the tip. The legs are greenish yellow. Winter adults show brownish streaking on the nape. California gulls breed in large colonies and feed on a variety of food, including fish, small mammals, and insects. The voice is a harsh squawk. The breeding adult is illustrated.

Western Gull, *Larus occidentalis*
Family Laridae (Gulls, Terns)
Size: 21"
Season: Year-round along the Pacific Coast
Habitat: Near-shore coastal waters, beaches, lagoons, harbors

The western gull is large and dark-backed, with relatively long pink legs and a large bill. As with other gulls, there is much variability in plumage throughout the western gull's growth, beginning with streaked and brownish plumage and eventually assuming crisp adult plumage. Adults have dark slate gray backs and wings with black primaries and white tips on the secondary and tertial feathers. The underside and head are pure white, and the bill is yellow with a red spot on the lower mandible. Winter adults have faint streaking on the head and nape. Western gulls forage on the water and onshore for fish, invertebrates, and refuse. Their call is a high-pitched series of loud *kyee!* notes. The breeding adult is illustrated.

Caspian Tern, *Hydroprongne caspia*
Family Laridae (Gulls, Terns)
Size: 21"
Season: Summer in northern California, year-round in coastal southern California
Habitat: Coastal and inland lakes and rivers

The Caspian tern is very large and thick-necked, the size of a big gull. It has a pointed, rich red bill that is dark at the tip, and a black cap on its head. Its upperparts are very pale gray, the underparts are white, and the primary feathers are pale gray above and tipped with dark on the underside. The legs are short and black. Nonbreeding adults have pale streaks through the cap. In flight, the Caspian tern uses ponderous, shallow wing beats and is less agile than smaller terns. It flies above the water surface searching for prey, plunging headfirst to snatch small fish, and may rob food from other birds. Its voice is a harsh *craw!* The breeding adult is illustrated.

Common Murre, *Uria aalge*
Family Alcidae (Murres)
Size: 17.5"
Season: Year-round on the Pacific Coast
Habitat: Open coastal waters, steep, rocky, offshore cliffs

Alcids are the Northern Hemisphere's version of penguins. The common murre is a sleek, thin alcid with a short tail, short wings, and a sloping forehead leading to a narrow, pointed bill. It is black above and on the head, and is white below, with dark webbed feet. In winter plumage, the white of the breast extends up to the chin and to the back of the eyes. Common murres dive and swim underwater, propelled by their stiff, short wings, to catch fish and squid. The voice is a rattling, muffled *murr* sound. They breed in huge, crowded colonies on steep, rocky cliffs. The nonbreeding adult (left) and breeding adult (right) are illustrated.

Mourning Dove, *Zenaida macroura*
Family Columbidae (Pigeons, Doves)
Size: 12"
Season: Year-round
Habitat: Open brushy areas, urban areas

The common mourning dove is sleek and long-tailed, with a thin neck, a small, rounded head, and large black eyes. It is pale gray-brown underneath and darker above, with some iridescence to the feathers on the neck. There are clear black spots on the tertials and some coverts, and a dark spot on the upper neck below the eye. The pointed tail is edged with a white band. The mourning dove pecks on the ground for seeds and grains, and walks with quick, short steps while bobbing its head. Its flight is strong and direct, and the wings create a whistle as the bird takes off. Its voice is a mournful, owl-like cooing. It is solitary or found in small groups, but may form large flocks where food is abundant. The adult is illustrated.

Rock Dove (Pigeon), *Columba livia*
Family Columbidae (Pigeons, Doves)
Size: 12"
Season: Year-round
Habitat: Urban areas, farmland

The rock dove is the common pigeon seen in almost every urban area across the continent. Introduced from Europe, where they inhabit rocky cliffs, rock doves have adapted to city life, and domestication has resulted in a wide variety of plumage colors and patterns. The original, wild version is a stocky gray bird with a darker head and neck, and green to purple iridescence along the sides of the neck. Its eyes are bright red, and the bill has a fleshy white cere at the base of the upper mandible. There are two dark bars across the back when the wing is folded, the rump is white, and the tail has a dark terminal band. Variants range from white to brown to black, with many pattern combinations. The adult is illustrated.

Greater Roadrunner, *Geococcyx californianus*
Family Cuculidae (Cuckoos)
Size: 23"
Season: Year-round
Habitat: Open fields, grasslands, urban areas

The greater roadrunner is a very large, ground-dwelling cuckoo with rounded wings, a long tail, a long neck, and a strong, pointed bill. It is heavily streaked overall, except for its pale gray belly. A pale blue patch appears behind the eye, and its short, shaggy crest is often raised. The legs are long and sturdy. Roadrunners run with their tails held horizontal and their necks outstretched, and rarely fly. They forage by chasing down reptiles, insects, and rodents. Call is a deep cooing. The adult is illustrated.

Barn Owl, *Tyto alba*
Family Tytonidae (Barn Owls)
Size: 23"
Season: Year-round
Habitat: Barns, farmland, open areas with mature trees

The barn owl is large-headed and pale, with small dark eyes, a heart-shaped facial disk, and long, feathered legs. Its wings, back, tail, and crown are light rusty brown, with light gray smudging and small white dots. Its underside, face, and underwing linings are white, with spots of rust on its breast. Females are usually darker than males, with more color and spotting across the breast and sides. The facial disk is enclosed by a thin line of darker feathers. Barn owls are nocturnal hunters of rodents, and their call is a haunting, raspy *screeee!* The adult male is illustrated.

Great Horned Owl, *Bubo virginianus*
Family Strigidae (Typical Owls)
Size: 22"
Season: Year-round
Habitat: Almost any environment, from forests to plains to urban areas

Found throughout North America, the great horned owl is large and strong, with an obvious facial disk and long, sharp talons. Plumage is variable: Pacific forms are brown overall, with heavy barring, a brown face, and a white chin patch, while southwestern forms are grayer and paler. Prominent ear tufts give the owl its name, and the eyes are large and yellow. The great horned owl has exceptional hearing and sight. It feeds at night, perching on branches or posts and then swooping down on silent wings to catch birds, snakes, or mammals up to the size of a cat. The voice is a low *hoo-hoo-hoo*. The adult is illustrated.

Burrowing Owl, *Athene cunicularia*
Family Strigidae (Typical Owls)
Size: 9.5"
Season: Year-round
Habitat: Open grasslands and plains

The burrowing owl is ground-dwelling, living in burrows that have been vacated by ground squirrels and other rodents. It is small and flat-headed, and has a short tail and long legs. Plumage is brown spotted with white above, and extensively barred brown and white below. It has a white chin and throat, and bright yellow eyes. Burrowing owls can be seen day or night perched on the ground or on a post, scanning for insects and small rodents. They sometimes exhibit a bowing movement when approached. The voice is a chattering or cooing, and is sometimes imitative of a rattlesnake. The adult is illustrated.

Anna's Hummingbird, *Calypte anna*
Family Trochilidae (Hummingbirds)
Size: 4"
Season: Year-round
Habitat: Woodlands, chaparral, streams, gardens

The Anna's hummingbird is compact, with a long tail and a thin, straight, relatively short bill. The male has green upperparts, dark gray wings, and a pale underside with green barring. The cap and throat (gorget) are brilliant, iridescent, rosy red, contrasting with a white eye ring. The female has a green crown and a pale throat with limited red feathers that sometimes form a central spot. Anna's hummingbirds hover to sip nectar from flowers or feeders, and sometimes eat small insects. The voice is a series of scratchy, rattling cheeps and chips. Males are very territorial and exhibit dramatic display behavior, swooping down and into a steep upward arc. The female (top) and male (bottom) are illustrated.

Belted Kingfisher, *Megaceryle alcyon*
Family Alcedinidae (Kingfishers)
Size: 13"
Season: Year-round
Habitat: Creeks, lakes, sheltered coastline

The widespread but solitary belted kingfisher is a stocky, large-headed bird with a powerful long bill and a shaggy crest. It is gray-ish blue-green above and white below, with a thick blue band across the breast and white dotting on the back. White spots are at the lores. The female has an extra rufous breast band and is rufous along the flanks. Belted kingfishers feed by springing from a perch along the water's edge or by hovering above the water and then plunging headfirst to snatch fish, frogs, and tadpoles. Its flight is uneven, and its voice is a raspy, rattling sound. The adult female is illustrated.

Acorn Woodpecker, *Melanerpes formicivorus*
Family Picidae (Woodpeckers)
Size: 9"
Season: Year-round
Habitat: Oak woodlands

The comical acorn woodpecker is loud and social, inhabiting big oak trees in large, busy colonies. Its back, wings, and tail are glossy black, and its rump and base of the primaries are white. It has a black breast bib below that dissolves in thin streaks to a white belly. The distinctively patterned head is black at and behind the eyes, whitish or very pale yellow on the forehead and chin, and red on the hind crown. Females have a black patch on the crown. Acorn woodpeckers eat mostly acorns, which they store tightly packed in holes they have drilled out. The voice consists of loud chattering squawks, as well as drumming sounds. The adult male is illustrated.

Downy Woodpecker, *Picoides pubescens*
Family Picidae (Woodpeckers)
Size: 6.5"
Season: Year-round
Habitat: Woodlands, parks in urban areas, streamsides

The downy woodpecker is tiny, with a small bill and a relatively large head. It is white underneath with no barring, has black wings barred with white, and has a patch of white on its back. Its head is boldly patterned black and white, and the male sports a red nape patch. The base of the bill joins the head with fluffy nasal tufts. Juveniles may show some red on the forehead and crown. Downy woodpeckers forage for berries and insects in the bark and among the smaller twigs of trees. The very similar hairy woodpecker is larger, with a longer bill and a more aggressive foraging behavior, sticking to larger branches and not clinging to twigs. The adult male is illustrated.

Northern Flicker, *Colaptes auratus*
Family Picidae (Woodpeckers)
Size: 12.5"
Season: Year-round
Habitat: A variety of habitats, including suburbs and parks

The common northern flicker is a large, long-tailed woodpecker often seen foraging on the ground for ants and other small insects. It is barred brown and black across the back, and buff with black spotting below. Its head is brown, with a gray nape and crown. On the upper breast is a prominent half-circle of black, and the male has a red patch at the malar region. Flight is undulating and shows an orange wing lining and white rump. The flicker's voice is a loud, sharp *keee,* and it will sometimes drum its bill repeatedly at objects, like a jackhammer. The northern flicker is sometimes referred to as the red-shafted flicker. The male is illustrated.

BIRDS: PASSERINES

Black Phoebe, *Sayornis nigricans*
Family Tyrannidae (Tyrant Flycatchers)
Size: 7"
Season: Year-round
Habitat: Open woodlands, gardens, shrubland—usually near water

The black phoebe is a long-tailed flycatcher with a relatively big head and a short, thin, pointed bill. Plumage is sooty black above, on the head, and on the breast and sides. It is white underneath, coming to a point at the breast. The crown is often peaked, and the outer tail feathers show a thin white stripe. Black phoebes perch upright and bob their tails up and down, and they voice a high-pitched, whistled *seep*. They fly-catch insects from a low perch, and are often seen hovering. The adult is illustrated.

Western Kingbird, *Tyrannus verticalis*
Family Tyrannidae (Tyrant Flycatchers)
Size: 8.75"
Season: Summer
Habitat: Open fields, agricultural areas

The western kingbird is a relatively slender flycatcher with a stout black bill and a slightly rounded black tail with white along the outer edge. It is grayish or greenish-brown above, pale gray on the breast, and bright yellow on the belly, sides, and undertail coverts. Its head is light gray, with a white throat and malar area and dark gray at the lores and behind the eye. There is a small reddish crown patch that is normally concealed. Western kingbirds fly-catch insects from perches on branches, posts, or wires. The voice is composed of quick, high-pitched zips and chits. The adult is illustrated.

Steller's Jay, *Cyanocitta stelleri*
Family Corvidae (Jays, Crows)
Size: 11.5"
Season: Year-round
Habitat: Coniferous forests, mountainous areas

The Steller's jay is bold, stocky, and crested, with short, broad wings. Its tail, back, wings, and belly are bright deep blue, while the mantle and breast are sooty gray. The black head has a thick, pointed crest. Inland races have white eyebrows and thin white streaks on their foreheads. The legs and bill are stout and strong. Steller's jays eat a wide variety of food, from nuts, insects, and berries to picnic scraps. The voice is a loud, raucous squawking, and they sometimes mimic the calls of other birds. The adult is illustrated.

Western Scrub Jay, *Aphelocoma californica*
Family Corvidae (Jays, Crows)
Size: 11.5"
Season: Year-round
Habitat: Open scrub oak, urban areas

The western scrub jay is long-necked, sleek, and crestless. Its upperparts are deep blue, with a distinct, lighter gray-brown mantle. The underparts are pale gray, becoming white on the belly and undertail coverts. It has a thin white superciliary stripe, the malar area is dark gray, and the throat is streaked with white and gray above a blue "necklace" across the breast. Flight is an undulating combination of rapid wing beats and swooping glides. Its diet consists of nuts, seeds, insects, and fruit. The adult is illustrated.

Clark's Nutcracker, *Nucifraga columbiana*
Family Corvidae (Jays, Crows)
Size: 12"
Season: Year-round
Habitat: Coniferous forests of high mountain areas

The Clark's nutcracker is a chunky, wily, crestless jay with long wings and a stout, thick-based bill. Plumage is gray or brownish gray overall, with black wings and a black-and-white tail. There is a prominent white patch on its outer secondary feathers. Its deep black eyes are surrounded by whitish areas, and it has a black bill. Clark's nutcrackers forage in trees and along the ground for pine nuts, insects, and fruit, but will also scavenge at picnic grounds. They walk with a swaying, crowlike gait. The voice is loud, harsh, rattling squawks. The adult is illustrated.

Yellow-billed Magpie, *Pica nuttalli*
Family Corvidae (Jays, Crows)
Size: 17"
Season: Year-round in central California
Habitat: Riparian areas, open oak woodlands

The yellow-billed magpie is almost identical to the black-billed magpie, but it is smaller and occupies only a narrow range, being restricted to the Cenral Valley and the central coast of California. It also has a yellow bill and bare yellow skin around the base of the bill and eye. This heavy, broad-winged bird has an extremely long, graduated tail. It has striking pied plumage, being black on the head, upper breast, and back; dark iridescent green-blue on the wings and tail; and crisp white on the scapulars and belly. The legs are dark and stout, and the bill is thick at the base. Juvenile birds have a much shorter tail. Magpies travel in small groups and are opportunistic feeders of insects, nuts, eggs, or carrion. The voice is a whining, questioning *mag?* or a harsh *wok-wok*. The adult is illustrated.

93

American Crow, *Corvus brachyrhynchos*
Family Corvidae (Jays, Crows)
Size: 17.5"
Season: Year-round
Habitat: Open woodlands, pastures, rural fields, dumps

The American crow is a widespread corvid found across the continent, often heard voicing its familiar, loud, grating *caw-caw*. It is a large, stocky bird with a short, rounded tail, broad wings, and a thick, powerful bill. Plumage is glistening black overall in all stages of development. It will eat almost anything, and often forms loose flocks with other crows. The adult is illustrated.

Barn Swallow, *Hirundo rustica*
Family Hirundinidae (Swallows)
Size: 6.5"
Season: Summer
Habitat: Old buildings, caves, open rural areas near bridges

The widespread and common barn swallow has narrow, pointed wings and a long, deeply forked tail. It is pale below and dark blue above, with a rusty-orange forehead and throat. The male's underparts are reddish-orange, while the female's are pale cream. Barn swallows are graceful, fluid fliers, and often forage in groups to catch insects in flight. They build cup-shaped nests of mud on almost any protected man-made structure. The voice is a loud, repetitive chirping or clicking. The adult male is illustrated.

Oak Titmouse, *Baeolophus inornatus*
Family Paridae (Chickadees, Titmice)
Size: 5.75"
Season: Year-round
Habitat: Oak and mixed woodlands, rural gardens

The oak titmouse is found only in California and southern Oregon. It is a small, plain bird with a short bill and a short, shaggy crest. Its plumage is pale gray or brownish gray overall, slightly lighter underneath and on the face. Oak titmice flit and dangle in foliage to feed on insects, seeds, and berries. They were formerly considered, along with the juniper titmouse, as one species, the aptly named plain titmouse. The adult is illustrated.

Mountain Chickadee, *Poecile gambeli*
Family Paridae (Chickadees, Titmice)
Size: 5.25"
Season: Year-round
Habitat: Mountainous woodlands

The mountain chickadee is a small, fluffy bird with a tiny bill, similar to the black-capped chickadee but with a white superciliary stripe through the black cap. It is grayish above, with pale gray or buff underparts, and has a black crown and chin patch. Energetic and acrobatic, the mountain chickadee travels in small groups, eating small insects and seeds gleaned from tree branches. Its voice sounds like *chick-a-dee-dee-dee*. The adult is illustrated.

White-breasted Nuthatch, *Sitta carolinensis*
Family Sittidae (Nuthatches)
Size: 5.75"
Season: Year-round
Habitat: Mixed oak and coniferous woodlands

The white-breasted nuthatch has a large head and wide neck, short rounded wings, and a short tail. It is blue-gray above and pale gray below, with rusty smudging on the lower flanks and undertail coverts. Its breast and face are white, and there is a black crown merging with the mantle. Its bill is long, thin, and upturned at the tip. To forage, the nuthatch creeps headfirst down tree trunks to pick out insects and seeds. It nests in tree cavities high off the ground. Its voice is a nasal, repetitive *auk-auk-auk*. The adult male is illustrated.

Brown Creeper, *Certhia americana*
Family Certhiidae (Creepers)
Size: 5.25"
Season: Year-round
Habitat: Mature woodlands

The brown creeper is a small, cryptically colored bird with a long, pointed tail and a long, down-curved bill. It is mottled black, brown, and white above, and is plain white below, fading to brownish toward the rear. The face has a pale supercilium and a white chin. The legs are short, with long, grasping toes. Its stiff tail aids in propping the bird up, like a woodpecker's tail. Brown creepers spiral upward on tree trunks, probing for insects in the bark, then fly to the bottom of another tree to repeat the process. Its voice is composed of thin, high-pitched *seet* notes. The adult is illustrated.

Winter Wren, *Troglodytes troglodytes*
Family Troglodytidae (Wrens)
Size: 4"
Season: Year-round
Habitat: Moist woodlands, streams

The winter wren is tiny, short-tailed, and plump. It is brown overall, with dark mottling and barring. It is a bit paler on the throat and breast, and has a distinct pale supercilium. The tail is commonly held cocked up and the bill held tilted up slightly. The winter wren forages through dense vegetation, searching for insects. Winter wrens are inquisitive and may be lured into view by imitating their high-pitched, buzzy calls. The adult is illustrated.

Rock Wren, *Salpinctes obsoletus*
Family Troglodytidae (Wrens)
Size: 6"
Season: Year-round
Habitat: Open, dry, rocky areas, deserts

The rock wren is a stocky bird with a short tail, large head, and a thin, slightly down-curved bill. It is grayish-brown above, with fine barring and spotting. Underneath it is pale buff to gray, with fine streaking along the breast and dark bars on the undertail coverts. There is a pale superciliary stripe above the dark eye. The pale brownish tips of the outer tail feathers can be seen when the tail is fanned. Rock wrens search around rocks for insects, flitting from rock to rock and often bobbing up and down. The adult is illustrated.

Golden-crowned Kinglet, *Regulus satrapa*
Family Regulidae (Kinglets)
Size: 4"
Season: Year-round
Habitat: Mixed woodlands, brushy areas

The golden-crowned kinglet is a tiny, plump songbird with a short tail and a short, pointed bill. It is greenish gray above, with wings patterned in black, white, and green, and is pale gray below. The face has a dark eye stripe and crown, and the center of the crown is golden yellow and sometimes raised. The legs are dark, with orange toes. Kinglets are in constant motion, flitting and dangling among branches, sometimes hanging upside down or hovering at the edges of branches to feed. The voice includes very high-pitched *tzee* notes. The adult is illustrated.

Western Bluebird, *Sialia mexicana*
Family Turdidae (Thrushes)
Size: 7"
Season: Year-round
Habitat: Open woodlands, pastures, fields

The western bluebird travels in small groups, feeding on a variety of insects, spiders, and berries. It is a stocky, short-tailed, and short-billed bird that often perches with an upright posture on wires and posts. The male is brilliant blue above and rusty orange below, with a blue belly and undertail region. The orange extends to the nape, making a subtle collar. The female is paler overall, with a pale throat and eye ring. Juveniles are brownish gray, with extensive white spotting and barred underparts. Man-made nest boxes have helped this species increase in number throughout its range. The female (top) and male (bottom) are illustrated.

Varied Thrush, *Ixoreus naevius*
Family Turdidae (Thrushes)
Size: 9.5"
Season: Winters along the Pacific Coast; year-round in far northern California
Habitat: Woodlands, brushy areas

The varied thrush is a reclusive, robinlike thrush with a short tail and a deep belly. The male is dark blue-gray on the back, crown, and tail, with blackish wings that are patterned with orange patches. The underside is rusty orange with gray barring on the lower belly; it is white at the undertail coverts, and is collared by a black breast band. The throat and supercilium are orange, and a black stripe runs from the bill through the eyes. Females are patterned similarly but are much duller. Varied thrushes forage on the ground or in the brushy understory for seeds, insects, and earthworms. The voice is a long, sustained vibrato whistle, repeated in a different pitch. The adult male is illustrated.

American Robin, *Turdus migratorius*
Family Turdidae (Thrushes)
Size: 10"
Season: Year-round
Habitat: Widespread in a variety of habitats, including woodlands, fields, parks, and lawns

Familiar and friendly, the American robin is a large thrush with a long tail and long legs. It commonly holds its head cocked and keeps its wing tips lowered beneath its tail. It is gray-brown above and rufous below, with a darker head and contrasting white eye crescents and loral patches. The chin is streaked black and white, and the bill is yellow with darker edges. Females are typically paler overall, and juveniles show white spots above and dark spots below. Robins forage on the ground for earthworms and insects, or in trees for berries. The song is a series of high, musical phrases, sounding like *cheery, cheer-u-up, cheerio*. The adult male is illustrated.

California Thrasher, *Toxostoma redivivum*
Family Mimidae (Mockingbirds, Catbirds, Thrashers)
Size: 12"
Season: Year-round
Habitat: Chaparral, dense thickets, foothills

Found only in California, the California thrasher is a long-tailed mimid with a long, down-curved bill. It is dark brown above and pale pinkish-brown below, with a slightly darker breast. The head has a light supercilium and throat, with darker streaking along the eye line and face. The eye is dark, unlike the similar Crissal thrasher, which has a light eye. California thrashers thrash about on the ground, tuning over leaves and soil with their long bills to search for food. The voice is composed of erratic, short phrases of raspy, high notes. They also mimic the songs of other birds. The adult is illustrated.

Cedar Waxwing, *Bombycilla cedrorum*
Family Bombycillidae (Waxwings)
Size: 7"
Season: Winter
Habitat: Woodlands, swamps, urban areas near berry trees

The cedar waxwing is a compact, crested songbird with pointed wings and a short tail. The sleek, smooth plumage is brownish-gray overall, with paler underparts, a yellowish wash on the belly, and white undertail coverts. The head pattern is striking, with a crisp, black mask thinly bordered by white. Its tail is tipped with bright yellow, and the tips of the secondary feathers are coated with a unique, red, waxy substance. Cedar waxwings form large flocks and devour berries from one tree, then move on to the next. They may also fly-catch small insects. The voice is an extremely high-pitched, whistling *seee*. The adult is illustrated.

Yellow-rumped Warbler, *Dendroica coronata*
Family Parulidae (Wood Warblers)
Size: 5.5"
Season: Year-round
Habitat: Deciduous and coniferous woodlands, suburbs

Two races of this species occur in North America: The "myrtle" form ranges across the continent, and the "Audubon's" form can be found west of the Rockies. The "myrtle" variety is blue-gray above with dark streaks, and white below, with black streaking below the chin and a bright yellow side patch. There is a black mask across the face, bordered by a thin superciliary stripe above and a white throat below. The nonbreeding adult and female are paler, with a more brownish cast to the upperparts. The longish tail has white spots on either side and meets with the conspicuous yellow rump. The "Audubon's" variety has a yellow chin and a gray face. Yellow-rumped warblers prefer to eat berries and insects. The male "myrtle" form is illustrated.

Common Yellowthroat, *Geothlypis trichas*
Family Parulidae (Wood Warblers)
Size: 5"
Season: Year-round
Habitat: Low vegetation near water, swamps, fields

The common yellowthroat scampers through the undergrowth looking for insects and spiders in a somewhat wrenlike manner. This plump little warbler often cocks up its tail. Plumage is olive-brown above and pale brown to whitish below, with a bright yellow breast/chin region and undertail coverts. The male has a black facial mask trailed by a fuzzy white area on the nape. The female lacks the facial mask. The female (top) and male (bottom) are illustrated.

Wilson's Warbler, *Wilsonia pusilla*
Family Parulidae (Wood Warblers)
Size: 4.75"
Season: Summer
Habitat: Willow and alder thickets, woodlands near water

The Wilson's warbler is small and lively, with a narrow tail and a short bill. It is uniform olive-green above and yellow below, with some olive-green smudging. The head has large black eyes and a beanie-shaped black cap. Females and juveniles have a greenish cap with variable amounts of black. Wilson's warblers stay low to the ground, gleaning food from the vegetation, or hover and fly-catch insects. The voice is a rapid series of chattering notes, or a quick *chip* call. The adult male is illustrated.

Spotted Towhee, *Pipilo maculatus*
Family Emberizidae (Sparrows, Buntings)
Size: 8.5"
Season: Year-round
Habitat: Thickets, suburban shrubs, gardens

The spotted towhee is a large, long-tailed sparrow with a thick, short bill and sturdy legs. It forages on the ground in dense cover by kicking back both feet at once to uncover insects, seeds, and worms. It is black above, including the head and upper breast, and has rufous sides and a white belly. It has white wing bars, white spotting on the scapulars and mantle, and white corners on the tail. The eye color is red. Females look like the males, but are brown above. The spotted towhee and the eastern towhee were previously considered one species, the rufous-sided towhee. The adult male is illustrated.

California Towhee, *Pipilo crissalis*
Family Emberizidae (Sparrows, Buntings)
Size: 9"
Season: Year-round
Habitat: Chaparral, riparian areas with thickets, gardens

Unique to California and southern Oregon, the California towhee is a plump, sedentary, ground-dwelling sparrow with a long tail and a short, conical bill. Its plumage is very plain, grayish-brown overall, with rusty-orange undertail coverts and dark streaking around the face and throat. The bird lacks the dark central breast spot found on the similar canyon towhee. The California towhee hops and scrapes through ground litter, searching for seeds and insects, and voices a series of clean, quick cheeps. It and the canyon towhee were previously considered one species, the brown towhee. The adult is illustrated.

Golden-crowned Sparrow, *Zonotrichia atricapilla*
Family Emberizidae (Sparrows, Buntings)
Size: 7.25"
Season: Winter
Habitat: Dense brush, woodlands

The Golden-crowned Sparrow is a robust, fairly large sparrow with a notched tail and a relatively small bill. It is brown above, with dark streaking and pale wing bars, and pale gray below, washed with brown on the sides and flanks. The head is gray, with a broad black supercilium below a yellow crown. Nonbreeding adults are similar, but have less black on the supercilium. Golden-crowned sparrows forage in thickets for seeds and insects. The voice is a high, clear, three-note song that sounds like *oh, dear me*. They breed on the tundra of western Canada and Alaska. The breeding adult is illustrated.

Song Sparrow, *Melospiza melodia*
Family Emberizidae (Sparrows, Buntings)
Size: 6"
Season: Year-round
Habitat: Thickets, shrubs, woodland edges near water

One of the most common sparrows, the song sparrow is fairly plump and has a long, rounded tail. It is brown and gray above with streaking, and white below, with heavy dark or brownish streaking that often congeals into a discreet spot in the middle of the breast. Its head has a dark crown with a gray medial stripe, dark eye lines, and a dark malar stripe above the white chin. Song sparrows are usually seen in small groups or individually, foraging on the ground for insects and seeds. The song is a series of chips and trills of variable pitch, and the call is a *chip-chip-chip*. The adult is illustrated.

Western Tanager, *Piranga ludoviciana*
Family Cardinalidae (Tanagers, Grosbeaks)
Size: 7.25"
Season: Summer
Habitat: Mixed and coniferous woodlands

The western tanager is a highly arboreal, brightly colored bird with pointed wings and a short, thick bill. The breeding male has a black upper back, tail, and wings, with a yellow shoulder patch and a white wing bar. The underside and rump are bright yellow, extending across the neck and nape, and the head is red orange. Females and winter males are paler, with little or no red on the head. Western tanagers forage for insects, primarily in the upper canopy of mature trees. They are usually difficult to see clearly, but their vocalizations, which consist of three-syllabled, rattling, high notes with changing accents, are distinctive. The breeding male is illustrated.

Red-winged Blackbird, *Agelaius phoeniceus*
Family Icteridae (Blackbirds, Orioles, Grackles)
Size: 8.5"
Season: Year-round
Habitat: Marshes, meadows, agricultural areas near water

The red-winged blackbird is a widespread, ubiquitous, chunky meadow-dweller that forms huge flocks during the nonbreeding season. The male is deep black overall, with bright orange-red lesser coverts and pale medial coverts that form an obvious shoulder patch in flight, but may be partially concealed on the perched bird. The female is barred tan and dark brown overall, with a pale superciliary stripe and malar patch. Red-winged blackbirds forage marshland for insects, spiders, and seeds. The voice is a loud, raspy, vibrating *konk-a-leee,* given from a perch atop a tall reed or branch. The female (top) and male (bottom) are illustrated.

Brewer's Blackbird, *Euphagus cyanocephalus*
Family Icteridae (Blackbirds, Orioles, Grackles)
Size: 9"
Season: Year-round
Habitat: Meadows, pastures, open woodlands, urban areas

The Brewer's blackbird is small-headed and dark all over, with a short bill and bright yellow eyes (in males). The breeding male is glossy black overall, with purple iridescence on the head and breast, and green iridescence on the wings and tail. During winter the plumage is not as glossy. Females are drab brownish overall, and usually have dark eyes. Brewer's blackbirds forage on the ground for seeds and insects, often while bowed over with their tails sticking up. The voice is a short, coarse *zhet,* and a longer, creaky trill. Brewer's blackbirds form large flocks in winter, along with other blackbird species. The breeding male is illustrated.

American Goldfinch, *Carduelis tristis*
Family Fringillidae (Finches)
Size: 5"
Season: Year-round in western California
Habitat: Open fields, marshes, urban feeders

The American goldfinch is a small, cheerful, social bird with a short, notched tail and a small, conical bill. In winter it is brownish gray, lighter underneath, with black wings and tail. There are two white wing bars, and bright yellow on the shoulders, around the eyes, and along the chin. In breeding plumage, the male becomes light yellow across the back, underside, and head; develops a black forehead and loral area; and his bill becomes orange. Females look similar to the winter males. American goldfinches forage by actively searching for insects and seeds of all kinds, particularly thistle seeds. The voice is a meandering, musical warble that includes high *cheep* notes. The breeding female (top) and breeding male (bottom) are illustrated.

REPTILES

Side-blotched Lizard, *Uta stansburiana*
Family Phrynosomatidae (Horned Lizards and Allies)
Size: Up to 6"
Range: Most of California except the Central Valley and northwest regions
Habitat: Dry, rocky, or sandy areas, grasslands, chaparral

The side-blotched lizard is common in the arid western regions. It is small, with a long, tapered tail, long toes on its hind legs, external ear openings, and a distinct fold of skin on the throat (the gular fold). Its color is generally brownish or gray, which can be uniform or interrupted with a variety of spots, stripes, or chevrons. There is a dark blue or black blotch on the sides of the body just behind the front legs, from which the lizard gets its name. Males also have gray-and-orange-yellow stripes on the throat and blue-gray speckling across the back and tail. These lizards are active during the day, basking on rocks or logs and hopping or running among rocks, searching for small invertebrate prey, including insects and scorpions. The male is illustrated.

Western Fence Lizard, *Sceloporus occidentalis*
Family Iguanidae (Horned Lizards and Allies)
Size: Up to 6"
Range: Most of California except for the far southeastern regions
Habitat: A wide variety of sunny habitats, including grasslands, woodlands, brushy areas

The western fence lizard includes several subspecies of varying color patterns, including grayish or brownish, with longitudinal striping, spotting, or a combination of the two. In California, these common lizards are sometime called blue-bellies because the males show blue patches on the belly and chin. It is a compact, long-tailed lizard with big feet, a blunt face, and scaled, dry skin. Solitary and active during the day, fence lizards scurry through sheltered areas or among trees, feeding on all kinds of insects and other invertebrates.

Northern Alligator Lizard, *Elgaria coerulea*
Family Anguidae (Glass and Alligator Lizards)
Size: Up to 12"
Range: Coastal California and the Sierra Nevada
Habitat: Cool, moist woodlands or fields

The northern alligator lizard has a stout body, a triangular head with a long snout, short limbs, and distinct grooves along each side of its body, allowing it to expand for breathing and feeding. The skin is greenish brown to bluish, with variable dark spots that may coalesce into bands or stripes. The belly is paler, with thin, dark stripes that run between the scales. Juveniles are very smooth (like a skink), with a wide, light stripe down the back and no dark bands. Alligator lizards are secretive, moving through and under logs, rocks, and dense brush searching for insects, eggs, or small vertebrates. If captured, the lizard may detach its tail or emit feces.

Collared Lizard, *Crotaphytus collaris*
Family Crotaphytidae (Collared and Leopard Lizards)
Size: Up to 14"
Range: Eastern California
Habitat: Dry, rocky areas

Also known as the "mountain boomer," the collared lizard is a chunky, colorful lizard with a large head, large limbs, a long, narrow, rounded tail, and smooth, granular scales. Its most distinctive mark is a black-and-white collar band on the back of the neck. Otherwise the color and patterning are quite variable, but usually these lizards are yellowish, tan, or blue-green with small spots on the body, tail, legs, and face, and light banding across the back. Breeding females show orange markings along the sides. Collared lizards leap from rock to rock, and run across open ground on their hind legs with tails raised, looking like quick little dinosaurs. To feed, the collared lizard ambushes smaller lizards and insects, which it subdues with powerful jaws.

Leopard Lizard, *Gambelia wislizenii*
Family Crotaphytidae (Collared and Leopard Lizards)
Size: Up to 15"
Range: Central and eastern California
Habitat: Arid, sandy, or gravelly areas with sparse vegetation

The leopard lizard is fairly large, agile, and stout, with a large head, large limbs, and a long, rounded tail. Its snout is long (shorter in the "blunt-nosed" race of central California), and its scales are smooth and granular. The color is brown to gray above, paler below, with variable markings depending on the region. In general, there are light crossbars along the back, and an overall speckling of dark brown "leopard spots" on the tail, head, and body. In cool temperatures the lizard's skin may become noticeably darker; during breeding, males develop reddish bellies, while females have reddish markings on their sides. Active during the day, leopard lizards scamper quickly along the ground and in brush, preying on insects and other lizards.

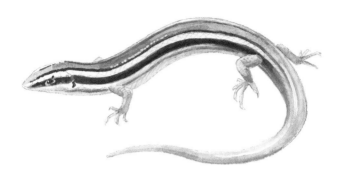

Western Skink, *Eumeces skiltonianus*
Family Scincidae (Skinks)
Size: Up to 9"
Range: Western and northern California
Habitat: A wide variety of habitats, including woodlands, streamsides, and fields

Like other skinks, the western skink has a long, narrow, cylindrical body, a long, tapering tail, small limbs, and smooth, shiny scales. It is distinctively colored, with a broad brown stripe down the back, blackish stripes along the sides, and pale stripes between these. The tail is bright blue in juveniles, becoming grayish in mature individuals. Breeding males develop orange markings under the chin and on the belly. Active during the day, western skinks usually stay hidden under leaves, rocks, or stumps. They feed on insects, spiders, sowbugs, earthworms, and other invertebrates. They will dig burrows and remain there for winter in cold climates.

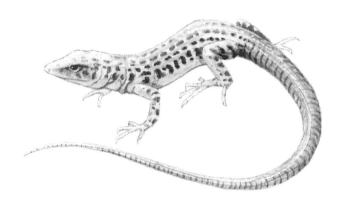

Western Whiptail, *Cnemidophorus tigris*
Family Teiidae (Whiptails and Racerunners)
Size: Up to 12"
Range: Throughout California
Habitat: Arid, open areas, open woodlands

Whiptails are known for their quick and jerky movements, relatively long, slender bodies, large limbs, and long, thin, whiplike tails. Several subspecies exist, with variations in color and pattern, but all generally show dark spotting or marbling on the head and body over a grayish, yellowish, or brownish background, with several paler longitudinal stripes down the back and sides. The belly and throat are normally whitish to pale yellow, but in some cases may be nearly black. The tail is blue in juveniles, fading to pale gray in adults. Active during the day, western whiptails feed on insects and spiders in leaf litter or underground. Wary by nature, they run rapidly to avoid danger, often seeking the protection of brush or burrows, and will detach their tails if attacked.

Rubber Boa, *Charina bottae*
Family Boidae (Boas)
Size: Up to 30"
Range: Northern California; isolated areas of southern California
Habitat: A wide variety of habitats, including woodlands, meadows, and streamsides

In addition to the rosy boa, the rubber boa is the only other boa native to the United States. Preferring cool, moist conditions, it has a stout, muscular body, tiny eyes with vertical pupils, a small, blunt head, and a thick, blunt tail tip that resembles another head. The scales are small, sleek, and smooth, giving the appearance of rubber. The color is unmarked brown, reddish, or greenish gray above and yellow along the underside. Secretive and docile, the rubber boa will burrow or hide under leaves, rocks, or rotten wood. It will curl into a ball with its head buried and tail exposed when provoked, almost never biting as a defense. Active during night or twilight, it moves on the ground, in trees, and it swims. It uses constriction to subdue its prey, which consists of shrews, other small mammals, and birds; it also eats eggs.

Common King Snake, *Lampropeltis getula*
Family Colubridae (Colubrid Snakes)
Size: Up to 72"
Range: Throughout California
Habitat: Quite varied, depending on region; desert, woodlands, wetlands, grasslands

The common king snake is a large, attractive, boldly patterned snake with several subspecies across the United States. All have shiny scales and some version of dark and light banding or mottling, which is composed of yellows, blacks, or browns. California king snakes usually have alternating bands of deep brown and white. Active during the day, or at night in warm weather, common king snakes feed on a wide variety of prey, including small mammals, birds, and even other snakes, which they kill by constriction. King snakes are so named because, although nonvenomous, they prey on venomous snakes without consequence, being mostly immune to venomous snakebites.

Western Shovel-nosed Snake, *Chionactis occipitalis*
Family Colubridae (Colubrid Snakes)
Size: Up to 16"
Range: Southeastern California
Habitat: Sandy areas of desert, arid scrub, rocky slopes

The small western shovel-nosed snake is restricted to areas of loose sand and gravel, which it deftly glides through and borrows into. The body is covered with smooth, glossy scales, colored whitish to creamy yellow, with fewer than twenty-one black bands or saddles, and sometimes with reddish-orange saddles in between. A black mask on top of the head extends between the eyes. The snout is flattened, with an overriding upper jaw, giving the snake a "shovel-nosed" appearance. Its eyes are dark and nonprotruding, and the belly is somewhat concave. It is active during the night or at twilight, searching for insects, spiders, and scorpions.

Gopher Snake, *Pituophis melanoleucus*
Family Colubridae (Colubrid Snakes)
Size: 48"–96"
Range: Throughout California
Habitat: Desert, pine-oak woodlands, rocky areas, scrubland, prairies

The gopher snake is widespread; this large, powerful snake has more than a dozen subspecies and goes by many common names, including pine snake, pine-gopher, and bull snake. Its body is thick, with ridged scales on the upper surface; the eyes have round pupils. The base color is light brown, pale gray, or yellowish, heavily marked with reddish-brown or blackish blotches and spots. Some varieties are nearly solid black; others have distinct, lengthwise stripes. Chiefly active during the day, gopher snakes hide in rodent or tortoise burrows, crevices, or under rocks, and often are found during the night in warm weather. They hunt on the ground, in trees, or in burrows for rodents and other reptiles, lunging at prey and constricting it. If confronted, gopher snakes will flatten their heads, hiss, and quiver their tails.

Common Garter Snake, *Thamnophis sirtalis*
Family Colubridae (Colubrid Snakes)
Size: Up to 40"
Range: Throughout California
Habitat: Well-vegetated areas near water, marshes, urban parks

The common garter snake is, true to its name, widespread and common, with more than ten subspecies that frequent developed areas and home gardens. It is a thin, medium-size snake with a head slightly wider than its body and relatively large eyes. The skin has keeled scales and is extremely variable in color, depending on subspecies, but always shows three longitudinal stripes—one running across the top to the back and two along the sides. Often there are blackish spots between the stripes. The underparts are pale. Garter snakes freely move from land to water; they feed on insects, aquatic invertebrates, fish, and small mammals. They are relatively harmless, but can bite and may emit foul-smelling fluid if trapped.

Sidewinder, *Crotalus cerastes*
Family Viperidae (Pit Vipers)
Size: Up to 31"
Range: Southeastern California
Habitat: Desert, arid mountains

The sidewinder is a relatively small, rough-scaled rattlesnake. It has the pit viper traits of a stout body, a wide, triangular, flat head, vertical pupils, and heat-sensing pits between the eyes and nostrils. It is also known as the horned rattlesnake because of the enlarged, pointed scales just above the eyes, which can be lowered to protect the eyes. The color is quite pale overall—some shade of cryptic gray, tan, or brown—with many small patches of darker color. Often a dark line is seen behind the eyes. Mostly active at night or during twilight hours, sidewinders otherwise hide in dens, vegetation, rocks, or burrows made by mammals. To feed, the snake awaits prey such as small mammals and lizards, and then quickly attacks using long fangs and venom. The common name comes from the way this snake speeds over sandy and fine soils with a sideways, undulating movement.

Western Rattlesnake, *Crotalus viridis*
Family Viperidae (Pit Vipers)
Size: Up to 62"
Range: Most of California, except the far southeastern regions
Habitat: Quite variable depending on region; forests, sand dunes, grasslands, rocky areas up to timberline

The western rattlesnake is a thick, rough-scaled, venomous pit viper with a flat, wide, triangular head, retractable fangs, and a tail tipped with horny segments that buzz when shaken. This species comprises several subspecies with variable coloration and size. The background color can be pale yellow, brown, reddish, greenish, or dark gray, with darker, light-edged blotches along the back that merge to cross bands on the tail. There is usually a pale stripe extending from the eye to the corner of the mouth. Western rattlesnakes are active most of the day except in very hot weather, when they retreat into burrows made by mammals. They feed on small mammals, reptiles, and amphibians, striking and biting the prey, letting the venom kill the victim, and later ingesting it. Much caution is advised around these snakes; although they usually avoid humans, if surprised they can cause a painful or lethal bite.

Western Pond Turtle, *Actinemys marmorata*
Family Emydidae (Pond and Box Turtles)
Size: Up to 8" (carapace)
Range: Most of California west of the Sierra Nevada
Habitat: Ponds, lakes, and streams with muddy bottoms and plentiful aquatic vegetation

The western pond turtle is a mostly aquatic pond turtle with a low, smooth, unkeeled carapace, an unhinged plastron, well-clawed feet, and a blunt head. The carapace is generally dark brown or olive, with thin, radiating yellowish marks or a marbled pattern—or it may lack the patterning and be plainly colored. The plastron is pale yellow; the legs and head are speckled in dark brown, black, and yellow. Males have a contrasting light throat, while the throat of females is dark. They aggressively defend prime basking sites but will leap to safely in the water at the slightest notice of an intruder. They are opportunistic feeders, eating most any available food, including aquatic plants, algae, insects, larvae, crayfish, and carrion.

AMPHIBIANS

Northern Pacific Tree Frog, *Psuedacris regilla*
Family Hylidae (Tree Frogs)
Size: Up to 2"
Range: Throughout California except the far southeastern region
Habitat: Streamsides, lakes, fields, meadows, and woodlands near water

The Northern Pacific tree frog is quite common in California. This medium-size frog is most at home creeping about vegetation near the ground. Its toes are thin and end in circular tips with pads underneath to aid in clinging to plants; the back feet are slightly webbed. The skin is rough and can be colored green, brown, or nearly black, with variable amounts of darker blotches on the back—but there is always a black stripe through the eye, and sometimes a dark triangular spot on top of the head. Males have a dark, extendible throat patch that inflates while singing. Interestingly, these frogs are capable of changing their color seasonally or within the course of hours. Hiding in leaves, logs, or rocks during the day, Northern Pacific tree frogs are mostly active at night, hunting for insects and small invertebrates.

American Bullfrog, *Lithobates catesbeiana*
Family Ranidae (True Frogs)
Size: Up to 6"
Range: Most of California west of the Sierra Nevada
Habitat: Ponds and lakes with dense vegetation

North America's largest frog, the bullfrog is squat and heavy-bodied, with massive rear legs that enable quick, strong leaps and swimming. Its smooth skin is green to brownish green, with brown or gray mottling or spotting and a pale belly. It has large external eardrums just behind the eyes. Bullfrogs are mostly nocturnal and are always found in or near a body of water. Their large mouths enable them to feed on a wide variety of prey, including insects, aquatic invertebrates, and even small mammals or birds.

Great Plains Toad, *Anaxyrus cognatus*
Family Bufonidae (Toads)
Size: Up to 4.5"
Range: Far southeastern California
Habitat: Prairies, desert scrub, farmlands, areas with loose soils and ephemeral water sources

The Great Plains toad is a large, plump burrowing amphibian that may spend much of its life underground, especially during dry weather. Two raised cranial crests atop the head converge in front to form a knob on the upper snout, while in back the crests diverge to the parotid glands. Its skin is rough, covered with small warts, and colored pale brown, gray, or olive, with symmetrically arranged darker blotches with light borders across the back. Its belly is unmarked white. Active at night, Great Plains toads eat earthworms and insects, especially the destructive cutworm that can devastate crops. In breeding season during summer rains, males vocalize long, drawn-out, high-pitched trilling songs.

Western Spadefoot Toad, *Spea hammondi*
Family Scaphiopodidae (Spadefoot Toads)
Size: Up to 2.5"
Range: Central Valley and coastal southern California
Habitat: Dry, grassy plains; sandy or gravelly areas

The spadefoots are so-called because they possess a small, hard, spadelike projection on the bottom of each hind foot, which is used to help excavate burrows. The Western spadefoot has a squat body, large, protruding eyes with vertical pupils, smoother skin than the true toads, and no parotid glands. The color is gray, brown, or greenish, with variable darker blotches and spots that sometimes form indistinct lines down the back. The spots often contain orange-tipped warts; the belly is unmarked white. Spadefoots remain in burrows during the day and in times of dry weather, emerging at night and during periods of rain to feed on a variety of insects and worms. They have a quick breeding schedule, suitable for producing young in temporary, seasonal pools. The skin of these toads secretes a chemical that can cause allergy symptoms in humans.

Tiger Salamander, *Ambystoma tigrinum*
Family Ambystomatidae (Mole Salamanders)
Size: Up to 13"
Range: Central California to the coast
Habitat: Quite varied; forests, grasslands, sageland, wetlands

The tiger salamander is the largest land-dwelling salamander in the world, with a wide variation in color and pattern. Its body is robust and rounded, with a broad, blunt head, small eyes, smooth, shiny skin, and a long tail (longer in males). There are six recognized subspecies, each markedly different in appearance, ranging from black or brown with yellowish crossbars or whitish spots to pale brown with black barring to pea green with black blotches. Tiger salamanders spend most of their lives in deep burrows made by rodents, emerging during late winter rains and migrating to pools or streams to breed. They feed on insects, worms, other amphibians, and small rodents.

California Giant Salamander, *Dicamptodon ensatus*
Family Dicamptodontidae (Giant Salamanders)
Size: Up to 12"
Range: Northwestern California
Habitat: Streams, lakes, and springs in cool, moist woodlands

Although smaller than the tiger salamander, and previously placed in the same family, the California giant salamander is still very large and imposing. Its body is thick, with a long, flattened tail, an oversize, blunt head and indistinct costal grooves. The smooth, moist skin is brown (sometimes with a violet cast) above, pale brown or creamy below, with variable dark mottling and blotches that sometimes forms a netlike pattern on the back and sides. Active day or night, and comfortable in water or on land, these salamanders hide under vegetation, rocks, and rotting logs, feeding on insects, other amphibians, snakes, and even small mammals. Although most salamanders are incapable of vocalization, this species can emit a low yelping sound when provoked.

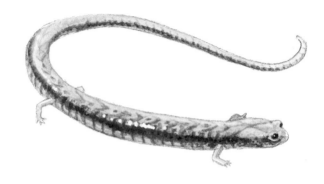

California Slender Salamander, *Batrachoseps attenuatus*
Family Plethodontidae (Lungless Salamanders)
Size: Up to 5.5"
Range: California coastal foothills north into southern Oregon; also Sierra Nevada
Habitat: Moist woodlands and fields, especially near redwoods

The California slender salamander is a small, very thin salamander with a long, rounded tail, a small head and eyes, and tiny, thin limbs. As with the other lungless salamanders, it absorbs oxygen through its moist, slimy skin and has distinct costal grooves along the length of its body. The color is gray-brown to black overall, with a paler wide dorsal stripe that varies from brown to reddish to yellowish, and is often marked with thin, darker, forward-pointing chevrons. Its belly is dark with fine white specks; the underside of the tail is creamy white. Especially active during periods of rain, slender salamanders lurk among leaf litter and moist logs or roots to hunt for earthworms, spiders, and other invertebrates. They are often found motionless in a tight coil, and then quickly and erratically squirm away, even detaching their tail to distract predators.

Arboreal Salamander, *Aneides lugubris*
Family Plethodontidae (Lungless Salamanders)
Size: Up to 7"
Range: Coastal regions and in the Sierra Nevada
Habitat: Oak and pine woodlands, sand dunes, marshes

Called the arboreal salamander for good reason, this species is an excellent climber, with expanded, squarish toes and a round, curling, grasping tail. As with others in this family, the arboreal salamander lacks lungs, absorbing oxygen through its skin, and has a small groove between the nostril and the upper lip. Its head is large compared to its body, and the jaw is laden with sharp teeth that can cause a painful bite. The color is brown above, with small, pale yellow dots; the underside is whitish, gray, or creamy. Arboreal salamanders stay in moist nooks in trees or in leaf litter, venturing out when the weather is wet to feed on insects, worms, snails, and occasionally other salamanders, which they snatch with their tongues.

California Newt, *Taricha torosa*
Family Salamandridae (Newts, Salamanders)
Size: Up to 7.5"
Range: Along the coast and in the coastal foothills; Sierra Nevada
Habitat: Woodlands of oak, redwood, and pine near streams or ponds

The California newt is typical of the newt family, with its generally dry, rough skin and lack of distinct costal grooves. It has a stocky body and is colored light brown to reddish brown above and yellow-orange below, with little contrast in between. The lower eyelids and eyes are pale. During breeding season, males develop smooth skin, a flattened tail, dark, rough patches on the inner thighs, and an enlarged vent (anal area). California newts lurk in leaf litter and burrows made by other animals, roaming farther during rainy weather, and seek a water source to breed. When alarmed, they present a defensive posture, raising their front end and tail to reveal the brightly colored belly and throat. They feed on earthworms, insects, and amphibian eggs.

FISH

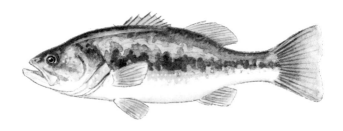

Largemouth Bass, *Micropterus salmoides*
Family Centrarchidae (Sunfish)
Size: Up to 29"
Range: Throughout California
Habitat: Shallow freshwater lakes, rivers, and ponds

The largemouth bass is a favorite of anglers for its tenacious fight when hooked. It is an elongate member of the sunfish family, with a mouth that extends to the rear of the eye, two separate dorsal fins (the first spiny and the second soft), and an indented tail fin. Its color is greenish-gray above, with a blotchy, blackish lateral stripe (fading with age), and a whitish belly. Largemouth bass skulk through warmer and weedier parts of creeks or lakes, foraging for a wide variety of aquatic prey including crustaceans, insects, other fish, and frogs.

Bluegill, *Lepomis macrochirus*
Family Centrarchidae (Sunfish)
Size: Up to 10"
Range: Throughout California
Habitat: Shallow lakes and rivers with aquatic plants

Also known as the "bream," the bluegill is a popular freshwater sport fish. It has an oval, highly compressed body with a small mouth, a dorsal fin that is elongated to the rear, and a slightly forked tail fin. Its color is grayish-green above, with indistinct, darker, broad vertical bars along the sides, and a dark blue-black patch on the operculum. The underparts are silvery to yellow, becoming red-orange on the chest of the spawning male. Bluegill feed on insects, insect larvae, crustaceans, and small fish. The male is illustrated.

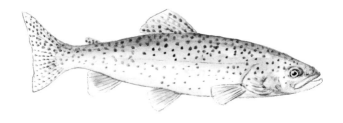

Rainbow Trout (Steelhead), *Oncorhynchus mykiss*
Family Salmonidae (Salmon and Trout)
Size: Up to 40" (usually smaller)
Range: Throughout California
Habitat: Cool, freshwater streams, marine waters

This species, as a member of the salmon family, has forms that exist only in freshwater streams (rainbow trout) and forms that migrate to the sea (steelhead). They are elongate, thick-bodied fish with small heads, soft fins, smooth scales, and a squared-off tail fin. Marine forms are blue-gray above, with white or silvery bottoms, while those of freshwater are greenish above, whitish below, with a pale pink section along the sides. Both forms have extensive black spots along the back, sides, and fins. Steelhead and rainbow trout lay eggs in the loose, gravelly bottoms of waterways, and the young either remain in their freshwater habitat or migrate to marine waters for a period of development, returning later to spawn in the same stream from which they came. They feed on a wide variety of prey, including other fish, insects, larvae, eggs, and crustaceans. The rainbow trout form is illustrated.

King Salmon (Chinook Salmon) *Oncorhynchus tshawytscha*
Family Salmonidae (Salmon and Trout)
Size: Up to 60"
Range: Northern California
Habitat: Cool, freshwater streams, open ocean, coastal waters

Of the five salmon species that occur in the northern Pacific, the king (or commonly, the chinook) salmon is the largest, attaining weights of more than 100 pounds. It is an elongate, robust fish with a squarish tail fin, relatively small eyes, and (in mature males) strongly hooked mandibles. Its scales are smooth and colored dark blue-green above, silvery along the sides, and white below, with irregular black spots on the back, dorsal fin, and tail. Spawning adults of both sexes develop a reddish-pink cast on their sides. Like others in the salmon family, the king salmon is anadromous, meaning that it is born in freshwater streams, migrates to the ocean, then returns to its natal stream again to spawn. The young feed on aquatic invertebrates and insects, while adults prefer fish. King salmon are a commercially important species, but highly susceptible to disruption of their freshwater habitats. The spawning male form is illustrated.

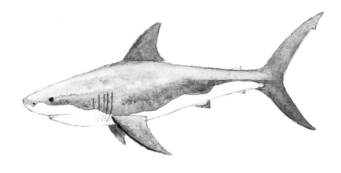

White Shark, *Carcharodon carcharias*
Family Lamnidae (Mackerel Sharks)
Size: Up to 20'
Range: Throughout coastal California
Habitat: Surface coastal waters, bays, near beaches and rookeries

Also known as the great white shark, the white shark is one of the most formidable creatures of the sea, and the largest carnivorous fish in the world. It has a massive, elongate body with a blunt nose, tall pectoral fin, and powerful, crescent-shaped tail fin. The mouth is laden with very large, sharp, serrated teeth that form rows. The color is gray above and white below—a pattern that provides camouflage when viewed from above or from below. These extremely fast swimmers patrol the coastlines in search of a wide variety of prey, including seals, seal lions, birds, fish, and other sharks, which they ambush and kill with fatal bites. Although attacks to humans are a regular (though fairly uncommon) occurrence, white sharks are generally uninterested after the first bite.

Bonefish, *Albula vulpes*
Family Albulidae (Bonefish)
Size: Up to 36"
Range: Coastal California south of San Francisco
Habitat: Shallow offshore waters, especially in estuaries with muddy bottoms

The bonefish is a popular sport fish, and a strong, swift swimmer in shallow waters. Its body is elongate, somewhat compressed, with a single, triangular dorsal fin, a strongly forked tail fin, a projecting, conical snout, and a lower mandible that is shorter than the upper mandible. Its color overall is silvery gray, with darker lateral stripes and faint barring along the sides. It has dark fins that are sometimes yellowish at their bases. Bonefish move landward with the rising tide to feed on small marine prey such as crustaceans, mollusks, and worms, often upending in the shallows to reveal their tail fins.

California Barracuda, *Sphyraena argentea*
Family Sphyraenidae (Barracudas)
Size: Up to 48"
Range: Coastal California
Habitat: Open seas, near-shore waters with sandy or muddy bottoms

The California Barracuda is a fearsome-looking tropical fish that is ruthless with its prey, but generally less interested in humans than most tropical barracudas. It has a large, elongate body with a roundish cross-section, and a pointed, tooth-laden mouth with a protruding lower jaw. There are two separate, pointed dorsal fins, mirrored below by pelvic and anal fins, and a large, forked tail fin. The barracuda's color is blue-gray above and silvery white on the sides and bottom, with sparse black spots on the sides. The young may form groups, but adult barracudas are generally solitary. They prey on fish by ambush, lurking and moving slowly before suddenly chasing prey with fast, direct swimming.

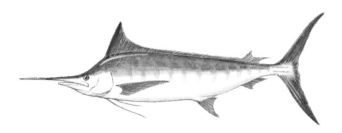

Blue Marlin, *Makaira nigricans*
Family Istiophoridae (Billfish)
Size: Up to 10' or longer
Range: Coastal southern California
Habitat: Offshore waters, generally near the surface

The blue marlin is a huge, streamlined, extremely fast fish, highly prized by sport anglers. It has a steep forehead and a thick body up front, which gradually tapers to a narrow peduncle (base of the tail) and tall, thin, curving tail fin. Perhaps most striking is the elongated, spearlike snout that overlaps the much shorter lower mandible. The dorsal fin is tall in front, quickly tapering to a narrow strip that extends along most of the back. Its color is deep blue to brownish above, white below, with pale blue barring on the sides. The abundance of blue marlin in the waters off California varies as they migrate according to the seasons.

Dolphinfish, *Coryphaena hippurus*
Family Coryphaenidae (Dolphinfish)
Size: Up to 50"
Range: Coastal California
Habitat: Offshore waters, generally near the surface

Also known as the dorado, or simply as the dolphin, the dolphin-fish is a large, marine sport fish renowned for its fast swimming speed and great strength. Its body is long and compressed, with a tall forehead (highest in males). A long dorsal fin runs the length of the back; the dolphinfish also has a long anal fin and a deeply forked tail fin that arises from a narrow peduncle (base of the tail). The color is striking, with hues of brilliant yellow or bluish-green along the back, dorsal fin, and upper sides, silver or gold along the sides and bottom, and small blue spots all over. These colors quickly fade upon death. Dolphinfish chase flying fish close to the surface, or congregate in beds of algae, feeding on smaller fish, shrimp, and crustaceans.

Diamond Turbot, *Pleuronichthys guttulatus*
Family Pleuronectidae (Right-eye Flounders)
Size: Up to 18"
Range: Coastal California
Habitat: Shallow offshore waters, generally with sandy or muddy bottoms

The diamond turbot is a flatfish whose eyes are both located on the right side of the body, which is the upper surface as the fish settles into its favored habitat of shallow, sandy or muddy sea bottoms. As its name suggests, the body is distinctively angular and diamond-shaped, with a short snout and a curved tail fin. The color above is grayish with blue spots (sometimes with a golden cast around the mouth area); below the turbot is pale and unmarked. It shimmies into the substrate, often in sloughs or estuaries, camouflaging itself as it feeds on worms, shrimp, and crustaceans.

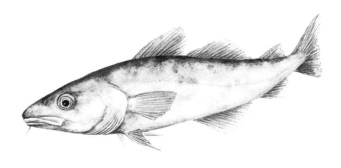

Pacific Cod, *Gadus macrocephalus*
Family Gadidae (Cods)
Size: Up to 44"
Range: Coastal northern California
Habitat: Near-shore marine waters, usually close to the seafloor

The Pacific cod is an important fish in commercial fisheries, and is commonly known as the gray cod or grayfish. Found near the ocean bottom, cod form large schools, where they feed on a wide variety of fish, cephalopods, and crustaceans. The body is elongate; the cod has a large head (as the Latin name, *macrocephalus,* indicates), a squared tail fin, three distinct dorsal fins, and a pair of thin barbels (whiskers) below the mouth. The color is brownish-gray above, whitish below, with variable amounts of dark mottling on the sides. The lateral line arches above the pectoral fin, then follows the midline of the body to the tail.

Surf Smelt, *Hypomesus pretiosus*
Family Osmeridae (Smelts)
Size: Up to 10"
Range: Coastal northern California
Habitat: Shallow offshore waters, surf zone

The surf smelt is a small, schooling fish often found near the shore or in the surf zone. They are considered a bait fish, along with anchovies and herring, because they are often utilized by anglers to catch larger fish. The body is narrow and somewhat delicate, with a small dorsal fin, a small adipose fin, a forked tail fin, and a short upper mandible that does not extend past the eye. The color is bluish-green on the back and silvery along the sides (sometimes golden in mature individuals), with a darker lateral line (quite pale in the live fish). Smelt patrol shallow waters for plankton and small invertebrates. They spawn in the sand, using a sticky substance on the eggs that adheres them to the bottom.

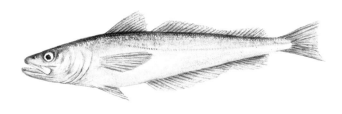

Pacific Hake, *Merluccius productus*
Family Merlucciidae (Hakes and Allies)
Size: Up to 36"
Range: Coastal California
Habitat: Offshore marine waters

The Pacific hake, also known as the Pacific whiting, is similar in shape to the cod, with an elongate body, a square tail fin, a double dorsal fin, and a lower jaw that projects beyond that of the upper jaw. The color is dark silvery gray above, with small dark spots; below is mostly whitish. Pacific hake occupy a wide range of water depths, from murky bottoms to near the surface, in search of a variety of prey that includes plankton, other fishes, and crustaceans. Although not commercially important as a fish for the dinner table, their soft flesh is often utilized for fish meal or imitation crab meat.

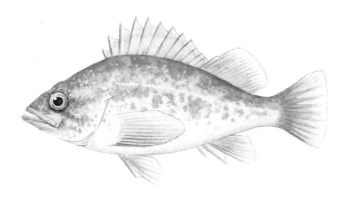

Kelp Rockfish, *Sebastes atrovirens*
Family Scorpaenidae (Rockfish and Scorpion Fish)
Size: Up to 18"
Range: Coastal central and southern California
Habitat: Rocky bottoms, kelp beds

The kelp rockfish, also known as the sugar bass, is one of many rockfish species found along the California coast. All rockfish have broad, compressed bodies, large eyes, spines on the head, and a dorsal fin composed of a front part with sharp spines followed by a section of soft rays. This species is cryptically colored brownish-green above, pale below, with darker brownish mottling on the back and sides. As its name suggests, it commonly lingers in the safety of kelp beds, where it feeds on a variety of marine invertebrates, crustaceans, and small fish, but it may also be found on the bottoms in rock crevices. It is a popular sport fish in California.

Cabezon, *Scorpaenichthys marmoratus*
Family Cottidae (Sculpins)
Size: Up to 30"
Range: Coastal California
Habitat: Rocky bottoms, kelp beds

The cabezon is a very large member of the sculpin family, which contains some of the tiny, cryptic fish found in small tide pools. Although fearsome-looking, the cabezon's skin is smooth except for some spiny rays on the dorsal and pelvic fins. The body is elongate, fairly compressed, with a small snout, large eyes, and a squared-off tail fin. Above the mouth and eyes are small, fleshy appendages (called *cirri*). The color is variably brown, greenish, or reddish, with extensive mottling that provides camouflage in deep rocky areas or among kelp beds. Strong jaws allow this fish to feed on crustaceans and shellfish. It is a popular catch for sport anglers.

Bocaccio, *Sebastes paucispinis*
Family Scorpaenidae (Rockfish and Scorpion Fish)
Size: Up to 36"
Range: Coastal California
Habitat: Rocky or muddy/sandy bottoms

The bocaccio is an inhabitant of dark crevices, the craggy ocean bottom and sandy depths. It is a fairly elongate rockfish with a narrow snout and an extending lower mandible, a concave forehead, a spiny front dorsal fin, and a squared-off tail fin. The color is grayish or brown above, with dark mottling; it is pinkish on the sides, with a silvery bottom and a prominent, pale, lateral line. The young will forage on planktonic material, while adults favor larger prey such as other fish and cephalopods.

California Sheephead, *Semicossyphus pulcher*
Family Labridae (Wrasses)
Size: Up to 14"
Range: Coastal central and southern California
Habitat: Rocky bottoms, kelp beds

The distinctive California sheephead, a type of wrasse, is a robust, bottom-dwelling fish with a tall forehead, a long dorsal fin that ends in a point, a squarish tail fin, and a blunt snout with prominent canines. Sheepheads have different appearances depending on the sex and age. Juveniles are deep red, with a white midline stripe and black spots on the fins. Females are uniform pink or brownish red, with a white chin. The males have a red midbody, a black head and hind end, and a white chin. Curiously, all individuals are female until later development converts them to males. They feed primarily on echinoderms and shellfish, using strong jaws and teeth to help crush prey. Both male and female are illustrated.

BUTTERFLIES

Pipevine Swallowtail, *Battus philenor*
Family: Papilionidae (Swallowtails and Parnassians)
Size: 3–5" wingspan
Range: Northern California
Habitat: Woodland edges, streamsides, open fields

The pipevine swallowtail is dark, medium-size, and active, with shallowly scalloped hind wings and moderate tail projections. It is poisonous to predators and thus often mimicked by other butterfly species. The upperside of the forewing is flat black and iridescent, while the upper surface of the hind wing is metallic blue (more developed in males) with pale, crescent-shaped spots along the base. The underside hind wing has large, orange, submarginal spots and retains the blue sheen of its upper surface. The body is black with small yellow spots along the sides, and the antennae are thin, with clubbed tips. The caterpillar is dark, reddish brown, smooth, and lined with fleshy appendages and orange spots. The caterpillar eats the leaves of pipevines and related plants. The adult feeds on flower nectar and nutrients from mud puddles.

Western Tiger Swallowtail, *Papilio rutulus*
Family Papilionidae (Swallowtails and Parnassians)
Size: 3–4" wingspan
Range: Throughout California
Habitat: Gardens, parks, riversides, forest clearings

Among the largest of North America's butterflies, the western tiger swallowtail is common throughout its range, is diurnal, and—typical of this family—has distinct projections, or "tails," on the hind wings. When alight and/or feeding, the wings may be seen to tremble. Both sexes are bright yellow above and show ragged black stripes, like those of a tiger, along the anterior forewings, and black marginal patterning on both fore- and hind wings. The first submarginal spot on the hind wing is orange. The underside is patterned similarly, but is much paler yellow. Females show bright blue posterior markings. Like the wings, the body also has black and yellow stripes. The caterpillar is brown to greenish, smooth, and plump. The caterpillar eats the leaves of trees, including those from the rose, magnolia, poplar and willow families. Adults feed on flower nectar and the salts and moisture from puddles.

Orange Sulfur, *Colias eurytheme*
Family Pieridae (Sulfurs and Whites)
Size: 1.5–2.5" wingspan
Range: Throughout California
Habitat: Meadows, fields, farmlands, roadsides

Also known as the alfalfa butterfly, this common butterfly is often found in dense, low-flying groups over alfalfa fields, where it is often considered a pest. The upper sides of the wings are yellow and extensively washed with bright orange. A wide, dark band occurs along the outer margins of both fore- and hind wings, a reddish discal spot appears on the hind wing, and a distinct, black discal spot sits on the forewing. The dark margin in females is broken by irregular orange markings. The underside is yellow with a red-bordered white discal spot on the hind wing, accompanied by a smaller spot just above it. The body is pale yellow below, darker above, and the club-tipped antennae are reddish. The caterpillar is thin, smooth, and green, with a pale longitudinal stripe down each side. This species is similar to the clouded or common sulfur, which has a lemon-yellow rather than an orange cast, and lacks the hind wing spot. The caterpillar eats alfalfa and clover. Adults feed on flower nectar. The illustration shows the adult male.

Cabbage Butterfly, *Pieris rapae*
Family Pieridae (Sulfurs and Whites)
Size: 1.3–1.75" wingspan
Range: Throughout California
Habitat: Open fields, farmlands, roadsides

Also known as the cabbage white or small white, the cabbage butterfly is a hardy, nonnative species introduced to North America in the late 1800s and now found across the continent. The upper sides of the wings are plain, creamy white with gray to black apical patches, and show a distinct dark spot at the center of the forewings and in the upper margins of the hind wings. Females have an additional spot on the forewing, below the first. The underside is pale yellow to yellow-green. Early broods of this species tend to be paler, with fewer dark markings, than late broods. The body is dark above, paler below, with long hairs, especially on the thorax. The antennae are thin and club-tipped. The caterpillar is pale green with thin, longitudinal yellow stripes and a delicate, bumpy-hairy surface. The caterpillar eats cabbage and other plants of the mustard (Brassicaceae) family, including *nasturtium*. Also known as a "cabbage worm," it is considered a major pest to crops. Adults feed on flower nectar. The illustration depicts the adult female.

Pine White, *Neophasia menapia*
Family Pieridae (Sulfurs and Whites)
Size: 1.5–2.25" wingspan
Range: Mountainous regions of California
Habitat: Coniferous forests to subalpine elevations

The pine white is small and white, with rounded wings. It is often found flying high in the canopy of pine and fir trees. The upper sides of the wings are creamy white overall, with a dark gray costal margin, a discal spot, and an outer margin broken by white spots. The hind wings have faint, darker lines along the wing veins; these are more pronounced on the undersides. The female's wings are paler than the male's, and the undersides are yellow-tinged, with thin, pinkish margins on the hind wings. The body is mottled white and gray, and the butterfly has thin, club-tipped antennae. The caterpillar is small and green with white stripes along the top and sides. This butterfly drops from a tree on a silken thread to pupate on the ground. The caterpillar eats the needles of conifers, especially those of Douglas fir, balsam fir, Jeffrey pine, and ponderosa pine. Adults feed on flower nectar. The adult male is illustrated.

Gray Hairstreak, *Strymon melinus*
Family Lycaenidae (Gossamer-Wings)
Size: 1–1.25" wingspan
Range: Throughout California
Habitat: Fields, open rural areas, disturbed sites

The swift-flying gray hairstreak is the most common hairstreak in North America. Hairstreaks are so-called because of the usual presence of thin streaks along the undersides of their wings. They also usually have one or two thin tails on each hind wing. The upper sides of the wings are slate gray overall (browner in females), with white margins. When there are two tails, they are uneven in length, and accompanied near their base by a large orange spot above a smaller black dot. The underside is pale brown-gray with black streaking, bordered with white and orange. The body is stout, grayish above and paler gray below; the butterfly has black-and-white-dotted antennae tipped with orange. The caterpillar is pale green to brownish, plump, and covered with fine whitish hairs. The caterpillar eats the fruits, flowers, leaves, and seedpods of a variety of plants, including legumes, mallow, and cotton, often boring into its food. Adults feed on flower nectar. The illustration describes the adult male.

Monarch, *Danaus plexippus*
Family Nymphalidae (Brushfoot Butterflies; Milkweed Butterflies Group)
Size: 3–4.5" wingspan
Range: Throughout California
Habitat: Sunny, open fields, meadows, and gardens. During migration monarchs can be found in almost any environment.

The monarch is large, sturdy, and long-lived. It is most well known for making one of the most incredible migratory journeys of the animal kingdom—its yearly flight to Mexico, in which millions of the species gather in discrete, isolated locations. The upper sides of the wings are deep orange, with wide, black stripes along the veins and black margins infused with a double row of white spots. Males have narrower black vein markings than females, as well as a small, dark "sex spot" near the base of each hind wing. The underside is marked as above, but the orange is paler. The butterfly's body is black, with white spots on the head and thorax and thin, club-tipped antennae. The caterpillar is fat, smooth, ringed with black, white, and yellow bands, and has black tentacles behind the head. The caterpillar eats the leaves and flowers of milkweed. Adults feed on flower nectar. Both store toxins from milkweed, which make them distasteful to predators. The adult male is shown.

California Sister, *Adelpha californica*
Family Nymphalidae (Brushfoot Butterflies; Admirals and Sisters Group)
Size: 2.5–3.5" wingspan
Range: Most of California
Habitat: Oak woodlands and adjacent streamsides

The California sister is a striking, medium-to-large butterfly with relatively long, narrow forewings. It was previously considered the same species as the Arizona sister (found in Arizona) and the Bredow's sister (found in Mexico). The upper sides of the wings are velvety black or dark brown, with a broad, white, medial band across both wings and a large orange patch at the forewing apex. Sometimes there are deep blue and reddish marks near the base of the leading edge of the wing. The underside has a similar pattern; in addition, stripes of pale violet-blue can be seen near the outer margins and bases of both wings. The body is black above, paler below, and has dark, oblique stripes. The caterpillar is thick and pale green, with long tubercles known as "horns." The caterpillar eats the leaves of various oaks, ingesting compounds that make it distasteful to predators. Adults feed on rotting fruit, tree sap, flower nectar (rarely), and moisture and salts from soil.

Painted Lady, *Vanessa cardui*
Family Nymphalidae (Brushfoot Butterflies; Ladies Group)
Size: 2–2.5" wingspan
Range: Throughout California
Habitat: Open habitats, gardens, fields, alpine meadows

The painted lady is medium-size, wide-ranging, and common. It can be found around the world, so it is sometimes called the "cosmopolitan." It has strong but erratic flight, and is capable of long migrations. The upper sides of the wings are pale orange-brown with extensive black markings. A black apical region on the forewing contains several white spots, and small blue spots may be visible at the inner base of the hind wing. The underside forewing is patterned as above, but the hind wing is mottled in earth tones, with a row of submarginal eyespots. The body is speckled light and dark brown above, is whitish below; the butterfly has thin, club-tipped antennae ending in pale dots. The caterpillar is blackish with pale yellow stripes, and is covered in fine hairs and bristles. The caterpillar eats a wide variety of plants, including thistles, nettles, burdock, hollyhock, and mallow, enabling it to thrive in most areas. Adults feed on flower nectar.

Common Buckeye, *Junonia coenia*
Family Nymphalidae (Brushfoot Butterflies; True Brushfoot Group)
Size: 1.75–2.5" wingspan
Range: Southern and central regions of California
Habitat: Open fields, meadows, coastal shores

The common buckeye is medium-size and common. It has pronounced eyespots, which are thought to confuse and deter predators. The common buckeye tends to remain on or near the ground, or in the low parts of vegetation. The upper sides of the wings are variable shades of brown, with each wing showing one large and one small multicolored spot. There is also a creamy bar near the apex of the forewing, two orange marks in the discal cell, and scalloped patterning along the entire wing edge. The underside is paler, sometimes achieving a rose cast, with eyespots still visible. The body is tan to dark brown; the butterfly has pale, club-tipped antennae. The caterpillar is mottled black, white, and brown, with dark stripes above, and is covered in black branched spines. The caterpillar eats the leaves, buds, and fruit of plantains, gerardias, and snapdragons. Adults feed on flower nectar, and moisture from mud and sand.

Mourning Cloak, *Nymphalis antiopa*
Family Nymphalidae (Brushfoot Butterflies; True Brushfoot Group)
Size: 2.25–3.5" wingspan
Range: Throughout California
Habitat: Deciduous woodlands, parks, rural gardens

The mourning cloak is a common butterfly with the angular, jagged wing margins typical of the tortoiseshells. The adult overwinters in tree cavities, emerging the following spring to breed. The upper sides of the wings are deep burgundy brown with wide, pale yellow margins. Inside the margin are light blue spots surrounded by black. The underside is dark gray with the same yellowish margin, though speckled with black. The body is stout and dark brown to blackish both above and below; the head sports thin, club-tipped antennae. The caterpillar is black, covered with spines, and has small white dots and a row of reddish spots along its back. The caterpillar eats the leaves of a variety of broadleaf trees, including willow, poplar, elm, birch, and hackberry. Adults feed on rotting fruit, tree sap, flower nectar (rarely), and moisture and salts from soil.

MOTHS

Polyphemus Moth, *Antheraea polyphemus*
Family Saturniidae (Giant Silkworm Moths)
Size: 3.5–5.75" wingspan
Range: Throughout California
Habitat: Deciduous woodlands, gardens

The polyphemus moth, a very large, common silk moth with a stout, heavily furred body, is named for the mythical Cyclops, Polyphemus, who had a single eye. The upper sides of the wings are light to dark brown overall. The forewing has a small, black-bordered, white discal eyespot, small black apical patches, a dark submarginal line, and a reddish basal stripe. The hind wing has very large black eyespots encircling yellow, and a broad, dark submarginal stripe. The underside is paler overall, with only a suggestion of eyespots. The body is brownish overall, above and below, and the moth's feathered antennae are more pronounced in the male. The caterpillar is bright green with a brown head; it is banded with thin yellow stripes and dotted with orange tubercles bearing thin, dark spines. The caterpillar eats leaves from a variety of broadleaf trees, including oak, willow, apple, hawthorn, and birch. Adults do not feed. The illustration shows the adult male.

Sheep Moth, *Hemileuca eglanterina*
Family Saturniidae (Giant Silkworm Moths)
Size: 2–3" wingspan
Range: Throughout California
Habitat: A variety of habitats including coastal areas, mountains, woodlands, pastures, and scrubland

The sheep moth, also known as the elegant sheep moth, is a silk moth of the West that can be found flying during the day. The wing pattern and coloration is extremely variable. Generally, it is rosy to pink on the forewing and yellow orange on the hind wing, with both wings showing large, central black spots, marginal streaks, and transverse bands. In some regions, however, the dark markings may be more extensive, reduced, or entirely absent. The undersides of the wings are patterned as the upper wing. The body is long for a silk moth, with a thin, yellow or pinkish black-banded abdomen. It has feathered antennae (broader in the male). The caterpillar is blackish, often with dorsal red spots and white lines along the sides, and has rows of highly branched orange and black spines. The caterpillar eats plants from the rose family (Rosaceae), *ceanothus*, willow, and aspen. Adults do not feed. The illustration shows the male.

Pink-spotted Hawkmoth, *Agrius cingulatus*
Family Sphingidae (Sphinx Moths, Hawk Moths)
Size: 3.5–4.75" wingspan
Range: Throughout California
Habitat: Open fields, gardens

The pink-spotted hawkmoth has long, narrow wings, a relatively thick, long body, and powerful flight. The forewing is cryptically patterned in an intricate design of gray, brown, black, and white, which forms perfect camouflage on tree bark when the wings are lowered. The hind wing is grayish with black bands and is flushed with pink at the base. The robust body, which has a pointed tail end, is a mottled gray brown with distinct pink spots along the sides of the abdomen. The antennae are long, pale, and feathered. The caterpillar, known as the sweet potato hornworm, can be a pest to crops. It is large, smooth, green to brown or nearly black, with pale, oblique stripes along the sides, and has a tail horn. The caterpillar eats sweet potato and jimsonweed. The adult feeds on flower nectar with an extremely long tongue (proboscis), which allows it to probe deep into tubular flowers. Adults can also feed while hovering.

Isabella Tiger Moth, *Pyrrharctia isabella*
Family Arctiidae (Tiger Moths and Allies)
Size: 1.75–2.5" wingspan
Range: Throughout California
Habitat: Open, deciduous woodlands, grasslands, gardens, parks

The Isabella tiger moth is common and medium-size, most often known in its larval form, the woolly bear caterpillar. The adult has relatively long, pointed forewings, which are light yellow-brown overall and sparsely marked with faint bars near the outer and medial sections. There are also variable numbers of small, dark spots on the interior and outer margins. The hind wing of the female is tinged orange to pink, whereas that of the male is pale yellow. The body is orange brown, with a hairy, tufted, upper thorax and dark spots along the upper abdomen. The moth has thin, pale antennae and black legs. The caterpillar is plump and covered with fuzzy, fine hairs. It is black with a wide, orange-brown central section. The caterpillar eats a wide variety of herbaceous and woody plants, including maples, clover, sunflowers, elms, and grasses.

SEASHORE
INVERTEBRATES

Hermit Crab *(Many species)*
Superfamily Paguroidea (Hermit Crabs)
Size: 0.5–4"
Range: Coastal California
Habitat: Shorelines, tide pools, coastal waters with rocky or sandy bottoms

Hermit crabs are not only abundant along the coast, but in pet stores and home aquariums as well. Many of the species that occur in California share certain common characteristics. They have hard carapaces, but the tails are soft, curled, and tapering. For protection, an empty seashell of an appropriate size is chosen, into which the crab inserts its tail. As the crab grows, it discards the shell in favor of a larger one. Hermit crabs have three sets of walking legs, two pincers, and retractable, stalked eyes. Nocturnal and quite social, hermit crabs gather in groups, may live on land or in the water, and scavenge for any available food and algae.

California Spiny Lobster, *Panulirus interruptus*
Family Palinuridae (Spiny Lobsters)
Size: Up to 12" or longer
Range: Coastal central and southern California
Habitat: Rocky coastal bottoms, tide pools

The California spiny lobster (also known as the California rock lobster) hides in rocky crevices on the ocean floor during the day and emerges at night to prey on various shellfish, echinoderms, and marine worms. Unlike crabs, the lobster has no pincers. It has two long, spearlike antennae that are used as sensory organs and, when rubbed together, are a sound-producing organ that may deter predators. Its body is robust, with relatively small walking legs and a powerful tail that can be contracted to provide a quick burst of speed. The lobster is prized by sport anglers and commercial fisheries. The lobster's color is golden to deep reddish brown, with stripes on the legs and mottling on the carapace.

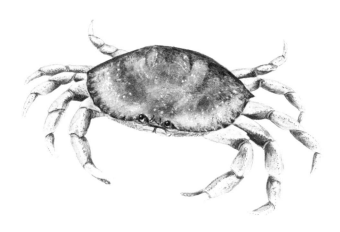

Dungeness Crab, *Cancer magister*
Family Cancridae (Rock Crabs)
Size: Up to 10" wide (carapace)
Range: Coastal central and northern California
Habitat: Near-shore muddy bottoms, eelgrass beds

The Dungeness drab is named for the town of Dungeness, Washington, home of the first commercial fishery for this large crab, which is prized for its tender meat. The carapace is wide, somewhat rounded, and smooth, with serrations on the front half. It is colored golden, reddish brown or purple. There are four pairs of strong walking legs and two pincer-laden legs for defense and grasping prey. The eyes are closely set and on short stalks. The crabs scavenge on the murky sea bottom or feed on fish and invertebrates, and settle into the mud or sand to conceal themselves from predators. As with many other crabs, the Dungeness molts its hard carapace to grow; for a period of time the crab is vulnerable until its new carapace hardens.

Pacific Mole Crab, *Emerita analoga*
Family Hippidae (Mole or Sand Crabs)
Size: Up to 1.5" (females larger than males)
Range: Coastal California
Habitat: Intertidal zone on sandy beaches

The ubiquitous Pacific mole crab (also known as the Pacific sand crab) thrives on sandy beaches in the zone where the waves wash in and out. Facing the water, they plant their hindquarters in the sand, and as a wave retreats they use specialized antennae to filter tiny bits of planktonic material into their mouths. When uncovered by water, they quickly burrow backwards into the sand to avoid predation by hungry shorebirds. The sand crab's body is compact and sturdy, with a tough, sand-colored carapace to protect its thin legs, eyes, and antennae. The tail can be brought up under the body for further protection. Females are typically larger than males, and can be identified by clusters or bright orange eggs on their undersides. Shore anglers are fond of these crabs as bait, as they are a favored prey of many fish.

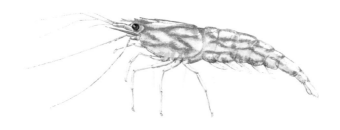

Red Rock Shrimp, *Lysmata californica*
Family Hippolytidae (Cleaner Shrimp)
Size: Up to 3"
Range: Coastal California
Habitat: Shallow to deep near-shore marine waters, especially rocky areas

The red rock shrimp is a member of the group known as cleaner shrimp, so-called because to feed they seek a host such as an eel, lobster, or fish, then pick off and eat bits of dead tissue or parasites. This is a form of mutualism, whereby both the shrimp and the host benefit from the shrimp's services. When a host is not available, the shrimp will scavenge along the rocky bottoms for bits of food. Its body is small, shaped like a tiny lobster, with thin, delicate legs and long antennae. The exoskeleton is slightly translucent, revealing patterns of red and pink. These shrimp are harvested commercially, used as bait by sport anglers, and are popular additions to saltwater aquariums.

Striped Shore Crab, *Pachygrapsus crassipes*
Family Grapsidae (Shore Crabs)
Size: Up to 2" wide (carapace)
Range: Coastal California
Habitat: Tide pools and vicinity, above-water rocks; estuaries

The striped shore crab is a small resident of California tide pools that can be found underwater, scurrying across the sandy beaches, or safely wedged into rock crevices on land. Having gills, however, they must periodically return to the water, and are never far from the sea. The crab's body is compact and compressed, with a trapezoidal carapace. It has widely spaced eyes, four pairs of walking legs, and a set of strong pincers. The color is variable, in shades of reddish purple and green, with distinctive black, horizontal stripes that give the crab its name. They eat just about anything they can find, including algae, decaying matter, small invertebrates, and even other crabs. Although fun to catch, caution is advised as the pincers (especially in larger specimens) can cause a painful pinch.

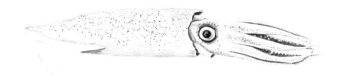

Opalescent Inshore Squid, *Doryteuthis opalescens*
Family Loliginidae (Pencil Squids)
Size: Up to 8" (not including tentacles)
Range: Coastal California
Habitat: Open to near-shore shallow ocean waters

The opalescent inshore squid is abundant and small-size. It is commercially valuable, and is also important prey for fish, birds, and whales. Its body is smooth and shaped like a narrow, tapered cone; the squid has triangular fins at the front, large eyes, and eight sets of dangling, suction-cup bearing arms, as well as two longer tentacles. Its color can change with environmental conditions and the mood of the squid, from bluish-white to translucent pale brown to deep red or golden, showing the spectrum of the opal for which it is named. All squid propel themselves by forcibly pumping water through a small, funnel-like opening below the eyes. Squid feed on a variety of marine animals, including worms, crustaceans, shrimp, and small fish.

Giant Pacific Octopus, *Enteroctopus dofleini*
Family Octopodidae (Octopodes)
Size: Up to 15' (including arms)
Range: Coastal California
Habitat: Intertidal zones to deep offshore waters

The giant Pacific octopus, true to its name, is very large and imposing. The octopus is found at all depths close to the California coastline. It has an oval to spherical head and eight, long, tentacular arms laden with suction cups on the underside. The skin is extremely resilient, and can change texture and color immediately to blend with its surroundings. The octopus feeds by stealthily approaching its prey, such as shellfish or crabs, inflicting bites from its bony beak, and injecting a paralyzing liquid. It is also equipped with a rasplike tongue that can bore holes into shelled prey.

Giant Green Anemone, *Anthopleura xanthogrammica*
Family Actiniidae (Sea Anemones)
Size: Up to 10" wide (including tentacles)
Range: Coastal California
Habitat: Rocky areas in the low to mid-intertidal zone, around pilings

The giant green anemone is common in tide pools, on rocky outcrops, and around wooden pilings all along the California coastline. True to its name, the anemone can grow to be quite large, with a thick, fleshy basal column and up to six rows of dangling, spreading tentacles. The color ranges from pale to brilliant green, blue green or olive, depending on the amount of sunlight it receives, since the tissue contains chlorophyll from algae that lives within. To feed, the tentacles detect and secure prey such as crabs, fish, or mussels, then secrete a paralyzing substance before the prey is ingested through the mouth in the center of the anemone's upper surface. Thankfully for curious beachcombers who like to touch the tentacles to see anemones close up, this secretion is not poisonous to humans. When water levels drop during low tide, the anemone closes up on itself to avoid desiccation.

Ochre Sea Star, *Pisaster ochraceus*
Family Asteriidae (Sea Stars)
Size: Up to 10" wide
Range: Coastal California
Habitat: Rocky intertidal zone, mussel beds

The ochre sea star is the most common large sea star of California's intertidal zone. Despite its name, this sea star can be found in beautiful colors other than ochre, such as orange, red, or purple (another common name for this species is the purple sea star). It has a broad central disk and five thick, radiating arms. The upper surface is hard and covered with small pale knobs, while the underside has tiny tube feet that allow for locomotion and assistance in eating. The sea star's favored prey are mussels, barnacles, and other hard-shelled invertebrates, which are pried open using the suction of many tube feet, and then devoured by the star fish's averted stomach, which is located at the middle of its underside.

Purple Sea Urchin, *Stongylocentrotus purpuratus*
Family Strongylocentrotidae (Sea Urchins)
Size: Up to 4" wide
Range: Coastal California
Habitat: Rocky tide pools and submerged rocky marine areas

The purple sea urchin is common in tide pools of the California coast. It is found low in the intertidal zone, preferring not to be out of water, and scrapes algae from rocks or collects tiny planktonic animals from the open ocean. The body consists of a rounded shell, or test, with many, long, purplish spines that aid in defense or in the collection of food. The urchin's mouth, on the center of the bottom surface, has a strong jaw and several teeth. Tiny tube feet on the test enable the urchin to move, albeit very slowly, to favorable locations, especially toward the bases of kelp beds. Purple sea urchins are a favorite food of sea otters.

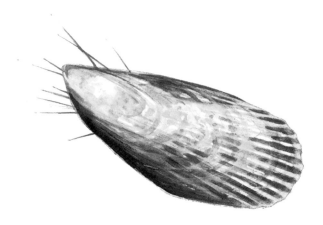

California Mussel, *Mytilus californianus*
Family Mytilidae (Mussels)
Size: Up to 8"
Range: Coastal California
Habitat: Rocky intertidal zones, deeper marine waters, bays

The California mussel thrives in the high-energy, rocky intertidal zone where strong currents and crashing waves are the norm. It is the most common mussel in this setting along the California coast, and forms huge aggregations, often in the company of barnacles. It is a bivalve, with two shell halves joined together by a thin ligament, and it attaches to rocks by means of thin, very strong threads (known as byssal threads). When covered by water, the shells open up to reveal delicate, hairlike structures that filter tiny organisms into the mussel for food. The shell is shaped like an elongated fan, with prominent ridges radiating from the base, and colored deep grayish blue or purplish, with a partial brown coating visible on some individuals. The inner surface of the shell is translucent blue and pearly white. Mussels are edible, but under certain conditions have been known to accumulate dangerous level of toxins.

Index

Accipiter striatus, 60
Accipitridae, 60, 61, 62
acorn woodpecker, 84
Actinemys marmorata, 134
Actiniidae, 189
Adelpha californica, 171
Aechmophorus
    occidentalis, 52
Agelaius phoeniceus, 116
Agrius cingulatus, 178
Albula vulpes, 151
Albulidae, 151
Alcedinidae, 83
Alcidae, 75
Ambystoma tigrinum, 140
Ambystomatidae, 140
American avocet, 67
American beaver, 14
American black bear, 22
American brow, 94
American bullfrog, 137
American goldfinch, 118
American kestrel, 63
American mink, 30
American pika, 5
American robin, 105
Anas acuta, 49
Anas platyrhynchos, 48
Anatidae, 46, 47, 48, 49, 50
Anaxyrus cognatus, 138
Aneides lugubris, 143
Anguida, 122
Anna's hummingbird, 82
Antheraea polyphemus, 176
Anthopleura
    xanthogrammica, 189
Antilocapra americana, 35
Antilocapridae, 35
Aphelocoma californica, 91
arboreal salamander, 143
Arctiidae, 179
Ardea herodias, 56
Ardeidae, 56, 57, 58
Arenaria interpres, 70
Asteriidae, 190
Athene cunicularia, 81

Baeolophus inornatus, 96
bald eagle, 62
barn owl, 79

barn swallow, 95
Bassariscus astutus, 23
Batrachoseps attenuatus, 142
Battus philenor, 164
belted kingfisher, 83
big brown bat, 3
bighorn sheep, 36
black oystercatcher, 66
black phoebe, 88
black-crowned night
    heron, 58
black-tailed jackrabbit, 6
blue marlin, 153
bluegill, 147
bobcat, 34
bocaccio, 161
Boidae, 127
Bombycilla cedrorum, 107
Bombycillidae, 107
bonefish, 151
bottlenose dolphin, 42
Bovidae, 36
Branta canadensis, 46
Brazilian free-tailed bat, 4
Brewer's blackbird, 117
brown creeper, 99
brown pelican, 55
brush rabbit, 8
Bubo virginianus, 80
Bufonidae, 138
burrowing owl, 81
Buteo jamaicensis, 61

cabbage butterfly, 167
cabezon, 160
Calidris alba, 71
California barracuda, 152
California giant
    salamander, 141
California gray squirrel, 9
California gull, 72
California mussel, 192
California newt, 144
California quail, 51
California sea lion, 43
California sheephead, 162
California sister, 171
California slender
    salamander, 142
California spiny lobster, 182

California thrasher, 106
California towhee, 112
Callipepla californica, 51
Calypte anna, 82
Canada goose, 46
Cancer magister, 183
Cancridae, 183
Canidae, 18, 19, 20, 21
Canis latrans, 18
Carcharodon carcharias, 150
Cardinalidae, 115
Carduelis tristis, 118
Caspian tern, 74
Castor canadensis, 14
Castoridae, 14
Cathartes aura, 59
Cathartidae, 59
cedar waxwing, 107
Centrarchidae, 146, 147
Certhia americana, 99
Certhiidae, 99
Cervidae, 37, 38, 39
Cervus elaphus, 37
Charadriidae, 65
Charadrius vociferus, 65
Charina bottae, 127
Chen caerulescens, 47
Chionactis occipitalis, 129
Clark's nutcracker, 92
Cnemidophorus tigris, 126
Colaptes auratus, 86
Colias eurytheme, 166
collared lizard, 123
Colubridae, 128, 129,
    130, 131
Columba livia, 77
Columbidae, 76, 77
common buckeye, 173
common garter snake, 131
common king snake, 128
common murre, 75
common yellowthroat, 109
Corvidae, 90, 91, 92, 93, 94
Corvus brachyrhynchos, 94
Coryphaena hippurus, 154
Coryphaenidae, 154
Cottidae, 160
cougar, 33
coyote, 18
Cricetidae, 16

Index

Crotalus cerastes, 132
Crotalus viridis, 133
Crotaphytidae, 123, 124
Crotaphytus collaris, 123
Cuculidae, 78
Cyanocitta stelleri, 90

Danaus plexippus, 170
deer mouse, 16
Delphinidae, 42
Dendroica coronata, 108
desert cottontail, 7
diamond turbot, 155
Dicamptodon ensatus, 141
Dicamptodontidae, 141
Didelphidae, 2
Didelphis virginiana, 2
Dipodomys ordii, 15
dolphinfish, 154
Doryteuthis opalescens, 187
double-crested
    cormorant, 54

downy woodpecker, 85
dungeness crab, 183

Egretta thula, 57
Elgaria coerulea, 122
elk, 37
Emberizidae, 111, 112,
    113, 114
Emerita analoga, 184
Emydidae, 134
Enhydra lutris, 25
Enteroctopus dofleini, 188
Eptesicus fuscus, 3
Erethizon dorsatum, 17
Erethizontidae, 17
Eschrichtiidae, 41
Eschrichtius robustus, 41
Eumeces skiltonianus, 125
*Euphagus
    cyanocephalus,* 117

Falco sparverius, 63
Falconidae, 63
Felidae, 33, 34
feral pig, 40
fisher, 28
Fringillidae, 118

Gadidae, 156
Gadus macrocephalus, 156
Gambelia wislizenii, 124

garter snake, 131
Geococcyx californianus, 78
Geothlypis trichas, 109
giant green anemone, 189
giant Pacific octopus, 188
Glaucomys sabrinus, 10
golden-crowned
    kinglet, 102
golden-crowned
    sparrow, 113
gopher snake, 130
Grapsidae, 186
gray fox, 19
gray hairstreak, 169
gray whale, 41
great blue heron, 56
great horned owl, 80
great plains toad, 138
greater roadrunner, 78
Gruidae, 64
Grus canadensis, 64

Haematopodidae, 66
Haematopus bachmani, 66
Haliaeetus leucocephalus, 62
harbor seal, 44
Hemileuca eglanterina, 177
hermit crab, 181
Heteromyidae, 15
Hippidae, 184
Hippolytidae, 185
Hirundinidae, 95
Hirundo rustica, 95
Hydroprongne caspia, 74
Hylidae, 136
Hypomesus pretiosus, 157

Icteridae, 116, 117
Iguanidae, 121
Isabella tiger moth, 179
Istiophoridae, 153
Ixoreus naevius, 104

Junonia coenia, 173

kelp rockfish, 159
killdeer, 65
king salmon, 149
kit fox, 21

Labridae, 162
Lamnidae, 150
Lampropeltis getula, 128
largemouth bass, 146

Laridae, 72, 73, 74
Larus californicus, 72
Larus occidentalis, 73
least chipmunk, 13
leopard lizard, 124
Lepomis macrochirus, 147
Leporidae, 6, 7, 8
Lepus californicus, 6
Limosa fedoa, 69
Lithobates catesbeiana, 137
Loliginidae, 187
long-tailed weasel, 29
Lontra canadensis, 26
Lycaenidae, 169
Lynx rufus, 34
Lysmata californica, 185

Makaira nigricans, 153
mallard, 48
marbled godwit, 69
Marmota flaviventris, 11
marten, 27
Martes americana, 27
Martes pennanti, 28
Megaceryle alcyon, 83
Melanerpes formicivorus, 84
Melanitta perspicillata, 50
Melospiza melodia, 114
Mephitidae, 31, 32
Mephitis mephitis, 31
Merlucciidae, 158
Merluccius productus, 158
Micropterus salmoides, 146
Mimidae, 106
Molossidae, 4
monarch, 170
mountain chickadee, 97
mountain lion, 33
mourning cloak, 174
mourning dove, 76
mule deer, 38
Mustela frenata, 29
Mustelidae, 25, 26, 27, 28,
    29, 30
Mytilidae, 192
Mytilus californianus, 192

Neophasia menapia, 168
Neovison vison, 30
northern alligator lizard, 122
northern flicker, 86
northern flying squirrel, 10
Northern Pacific tree
    frog, 136

northern pintail, 49
northern river otter, 26
Nucifraga columbiana, 92
Nycticorax nycticorax, 58
Nymphalidae, 170, 171, 172, 173, 174
Nymphalis antiopa, 174

oak titmouse, 96
Ochotona princes, 5
Ochotonidae, 5
ochre sea star, 190
Octopodidae, 188
Odocoileus hemionus, 38
Odocoileus virginianus, 39
Odontophoridae, 51
Oncorhynchus mykiss, 148
Oncorhynchus tshawytscha, 149
opalescent inshore squid, 187
orange sulfur, 166
Ord's kangaroo rat, 15
Osmeridae, 157
Otariidae, 43
Otospermophilus beecheyi, 12
Ovis canadensis, 36

Pachygrapsus crassipes, 186
Pacific cod, 156
Pacific mole crab, 184
Pacific hake, 158
painted lady, 172
Palinuridae, 182
Panulirus interruptus, 182
Papilio rutulus, 165
Papilionidae, 164, 165
Paridae, 96, 97
Parulidae, 108, 109, 110
Pelecanidae, 55
Pelecanus occidentalis, 55
Peromyscus maniculatus, 16
Phalacrocoracidae, 54
Phalacrocorax auritus, 54
Phoca vitulina, 44
Phocidae, 44
Phrynosomatidae, 120
Pica nuttalli, 93
Picidae, 84, 85, 86
Picoides pubescens, 85
pied-billed grebe, 53
Pieridae, 166, 167, 178
Pieris rapae, 167

pigeon, 77
pine white, 168
pink-spotted hawkmoth, 178
pipevine swallowtail, 164
Pipilo crissalis, 112
Pipilo maculates, 111
Piranga ludoviciana, 115
Pisaster ochraceus, 190
Pituophis melanoleucus, 130
Plethodontidae, 142, 143
Pleuronectidae, 155
Pleuronichthys guttulatus, 155
Podicipedidae, 52, 53
Podilymbus podiceps, 53
Poecile gambeli, 98
polyphemus moth, 176
porcupine, 17
Procyon lotor, 24
Procyonidae, 23, 24
pronghorn, 35
Psuedacris regilla, 136
Puma concolor, 33
purple sea urchin, 191
Pyrrharctia isabella, 179

raccoon, 24
rainbow trout, 148
Ranidae, 137
Recurvirostra americana, 67
Recurvirostridae, 67
red fox, 20
red rock shrimp, 185
red-tailed hawk, 61
red-winged blackbird, 116
Regulidae, 102
Regulus satrapa, 102
ringtail, 23
rock dove, 77
rock wren, 101
rubber boa, 127
ruddy turnstone, 70

Salamandridae, 144
Salmonidae, 148, 149
Salpinctes obsoletus, 101
sanderling, 71
sandhill crane, 64
Saturniidae, 176, 177
Sayornis nigricans, 88
Scaphiopodidae, 139
Sceloporus occidentalis, 121
Scincidae, 125

Sciuridae, 9, 10, 11, 12, 13
Sciurus griseus, 9
Scolopacidae, 68, 69, 70, 71
Scorpaenichthys marmoratus, 160
Scorpaenidae, 159, 161
sea otter, 25
Sebastes atrovirens, 159
Sebastes paucispinis, 161
Semicossyphus pulcher, 162
sharp-shinned hawk, 60
sheep moth, 177
shore crabs, 186
Sialia mexicana, 103
side-blotched lizard, 120
sidewinder, 132
sisters butterflies group, 171
Sitta carolinensis, 98
Sittidae, 98
snow goose, 47
snowy egret, 57
song sparrow, 114
Spea hammondi, 139
Sphingidae, 178
Sphyraena argentea, 152
Sphyraenidae, 152
Spilogale gracilis, 32
spotted towhee, 111
steelhead, 148
Steller's jay, 90
Stongylocentrotus purpuratus, 191
Strigidae, 80, 81
striped shore crab, 186
striped skunk, 31
Strongylocentrotidae, 191
Strymon melinus, 169
Suidae, 40
super paguroidea, 181
surf scoter, 50
surf smelt, 157
Sus scrofa, 40
Sylvilagus audubonii, 7
Sylvilagus bachmani, 8

Tadarida brasiliensis, 4
Tamias minimus, 13
Taricha torosa, 144
Teiidae, 126
Thamnophis sirtalis, 131
tiger salamander, 140
Toxostoma redivivum, 106
Tringa semipalmatus, 68
Trochilidae, 82

Troglodytes troglodytes, 100
Troglodytidae, 100, 101
Turdidae, 103, 104, 105
Turdus migratorius, 105
turkey vulture, 59
Tursiops truncates, 42
Tyrannidae, 88, 89
Tyrannus verticalis, 89
Tyto alba, 79
Tytonidae, 79

Uria aalge, 75
Urocyon cinereoargenteus, 19
Ursidae, 22
Ursus americanus, 22
Uta stansburiana, 120

Vanessa cardui, 172
varied thrush, 104
Vespertilionidae, 3
Viperidae, 132, 133

Virginia opossum, 2
Vulpes macrotis, 21
Vulpes vulpes, 20

wapiti, 37
western bluebird, 103
western fence lizard, 121
western gray squirrel, 9
western grebe, 52
western gull, 73
western kingbird, 89
western pond turtle, 134
western rattlesnake, 133
western scrub jay, 91
western shovel-nosed
   snake, 129
western skink, 125
western spadefoot toad, 139
western spotted skunk, 32
western tanager, 115

western tiger
   swallowtail, 165
western whiptail, 126
white shark, 150
white-breasted nuthatch, 98
white-tailed deer, 39
wild boar, 40
willet, 68
Wilson's warbler, 110
Wilsonia pusilla, 110
winter wren, 100

yellow-bellied marmot, 11
yellow-billed magpie, 93
yellow-rumped warbler, 108

Zalophus californianus, 43
Zenaida macrour, 76
Zonotrichia atricapilla, 113

About the Author/Illustrator

Todd Telander is a naturalist/illustrator/
artist living in Walla Walla, Washington.
He has studied and illustrated wildlife
since 1989, while living in California,
Colorado, New Mexico, and Washington. He graduated from the University
of California Santa Cruz with degrees
in biology, environmental studies, and
scientific illustration, and has since
illustrated numerous books and other
publications, including books in the

FalconGuides' Scats and Tracks series. His wife, Kirsten Telander, is
a writer, and they have two sons, Miles and Oliver. His work can be
viewed online at toddtelander.com.